THE AJAX DILEMMA

THE AJAX DILEMMA
Justice, Fairness, and Rewards

Paul Woodruff

With an Afterword by C. Cale McDowell

OXFORD
UNIVERSITY PRESS

OXFORD

UNIVERSITY PRESS

Oxford University Press is a department of the University of Oxford.
It furthers the University's objective of excellence in research, scholarship,
and education by publishing worldwide.

Oxford   New York

Auckland   Cape Town   Dar es Salaam   Hong Kong   Karachi
Kuala Lumpur   Madrid   Melbourne   Mexico City   Nairobi
New Delhi   Shanghai   Taipei   Toronto

With offices in

Argentina   Austria   Brazil   Chile   Czech Republic   France   Greece
Guatemala   Hungary   Italy   Japan   Poland   Portugal   Singapore
South Korea   Switzerland   Thailand   Turkey   Ukraine   Vietnam

Oxford is a registered trade mark of Oxford University Press
in the UK and certain other countries.

Published in the United States of America by
Oxford University Press
198 Madison Avenue, New York, NY 10016

Library of Congress Cataloging-in-Publication Data
Woodruff, Paul, 1943–
The Ajax dilemma : justice, fairness, and rewards / Paul Woodruff.
p.   cm.
Includes bibliographical references.
ISBN 978-0-19-976861-5 (hardcover); 978-0-19-935688-1 (paperback)
1. Fairness.   2. Justice.   3. Reward (Ethics)
4. Leadership.   I. Title.
BJ1533.F2W66 2011
170—dc22   2010053101

1 3 5 7 9 8 6 4 2

Printed in the United States of America
on acid-free paper

For Reuben McDaniel

*Without friends, no one would choose to live, even
if he had every other good thing:.... And for those who
are friends, there is no need for justice, but people who
have justice still need friends.*
　　　　　　　　　　　　　　　　—Aristotle, Ethics *8.1*

TABLE OF CONTENTS

PREFACE

You probably know an Ajax. He works hard, has many friends. He is loyal to his friends and to the people he works for. He is tough and courageous, and when you ask him to help, he is always there. You want to have him with you in a crisis.

You probably also know an Odysseus. He is so smart he's scary. He can talk a blue streak and charm the pants off anyone who does not know him. He's always coming up with new ideas, and you want him in the tent when you are trying to outthink the enemy. But you don't quite trust him. His values seem to slide around to suit his needs. You can depend on him to look after himself. But Ajax always looks after *us*.

When an Ajax competes with an Odysseus, Odysseus usually walks off with the spoils, leaving Ajax feeling he has been suckered. An ancient story tells one way this can happen, after they have been fighting in the Greek army outside Troy for nine years. Achilles is dead, the great Achilles. A god had made his armor out of precious metal, Hephaestus, the brilliant craftsman and artist. This armor is a treasure beyond price, and it is slated to go to the most valuable soldier in the Greek army. Will it be Ajax or Odysseus?

Ajax and Odysseus are engaged in a classic contest—loyalty and brawn versus brains and trickery. Which one of them makes the most valuable contribution to the army? Ajax loses, and he cannot bring himself to accept the result. Now that he has lost, he sees for the first time that the others have taken advantage of him all along, for the nine years of this war. He is monstrously angry; his anger explodes his position in the army, destroys his life, shatters his family, and puts his reputation into danger.

The issue is rewards. Rewards mark the difference between winners and losers. Rewards are public recognition for contributions made. They express the values of a community: Which does it value more, cleverness or hard work? Strength or intelligence? Loyalty or inventiveness? Does a university care more about teaching or research? Does a business care more about design or marketing? Look at who gets the rewards, and you know the values of the community. Rewards bring honor to those who are chosen for them; those who are not will feel anger or shame if they are denied the rewards they feel they deserve.

We see contests like this all around us. In industry, bankers and fund managers have carried off the prizes, while most of us are Ajaxes, team players who work hard at our various tasks and are loyal to the communities in which we live. In universities, hardworking teachers are often denied rewards, while stars of research may turn away from their students, earn fame for their scholarly work, and claim fat raises. When we see rewards going to others who do not live by our values, we feel that this cannot be right. We Ajaxes have been tricked. Justice, we feel, has failed.

Perhaps it has to fail. If Odysseus did not get the reward he wants, then he might quit, and there is no replacing him. He is crooked enough he might even go over to the Trojans. He has the only mind that could invent the Trojan Horse, a masterpiece of deception, and deception is the only way to beat Troy. If he were a banker, he might have the only mind that could invent a derivative investment vehicle more profitable for the short term than that of the competing bank.

Remember the Trojan Horse? A huge sculpture of wood made by the Greeks, which (along with a false story Odysseus had planted) fascinated the Trojans. They took it inside their walls. There were Greek soldiers concealed in its belly. They came out at night and opened the city gates to their army. And so Troy ended in flames and a sea of blood, all because it fell for the Trojan Horse. The Greeks triumphed through Odysseus's stratagem.

But for Ajax, justice fails, and when justice fails for an Ajax, he stops working, or at least the heart goes out of his work. He works slow, or he sabotages the team, or he is often ill, and his illness infects other members of the team. Everyone hears his complaints, and many share his sense of injustice. When Ajax stops or slows, important work stops or slows with him, especially if he is the lead workhorse on his team. In an extreme case, an Ajax can do serious damage to the team. Of course, an Ajax can be replaced if management realizes that he has become a problem. There are many Ajaxes looking for work.

In this story, the king's advisers tell him that Ajax might quit the army. This would be expensive because Ajax is worth four ordinary men. But the king says, "Sign on four new ordinary men." The king ought to remember, however, that these four new men will also need to have their contributions recognized in the long run. High turnover does not solve the Ajax dilemma.

Justice is what ought to have kept Ajax on the team, or, more generally, justice is what ought to keep any community together through the stress of disputes. Justice, ideally, does more than merely decide a dispute; justice makes disputes go away—or at least go far enough away that a team can continue working together.

Justice is precisely what we need to prevent conflicts like this from destroying us. We need it in our communities in order to make just decisions; we need it in our own hearts if we are to accept justice when it is done—especially when it is not done to our liking.

What is justice? We will see that justice is not a set of rules. It is not even the same as fairness. It is a matter of character and leadership. Justice belongs in the heart of each of us and in the soul of our community.

I cannot do justice to this subject in a philosophical treatise. Heart and soul reveal themselves in stories. What sounds good in a philosophical argument may look terrible in a real-life situation. When philosophers write about justice, they usually make ideal assumptions. They write up ideas that might work if all of us were rational, if we were all able to put evidence and logic ahead of emotion. Maybe we should all try to be rational, but the truth is that we are not. Justice is about giving people what is due to them. Inside a person, inside myself, justice is about giving due respect to each part of myself. And that includes the parts of me that are driven by emotion.

That is why I begin this book by telling the famous story. Part I sets up the story, part II tells it from four different points of view, part III reflects on the story, and part IV develops the conclusions with more rigor. If you prefer to begin with that, skip to part IV.

ACKNOWLEDGMENTS

It is fair and just to acknowledge the help of many friends, advisers, and teachers. Philip Bobbitt got me started by asking me on a public occasion what I would write next if I could. Thinking fast, I said, "Ajax." My graduate seminar on Sophocles had just chewed over this brilliant play, and several students had stirred up my ideas about it, most notably Dhananjay Jagannathan, David Riesbeck, and Matthew Kruebbe. All of us had been excited by Peter Meineck's splendid translation.

On issues related to fairness and management I owe a huge debt to Reuben McDaniel, colleague and friend, for many breakfast conversations. On justice and Plato, my teacher John Lucas at Merton College influenced me more than he could know, and recent conversations with Ruth Marcus have been most valuable. Betty Sue Flowers read an early version and was generous with advice. Former student David Niño helped me to a number of useful books on management. Sam Naifeh read the manuscript and helped with suggestions. Captain Don Inbody (USN, retired) helped me understand the consequences of promotion systems in the military. Edwin Allaire and Jonathan Dancy helped me understand what I was saying about the difference between fairness and justice. Jonathan Dancy's elegant work has had an enormous influence on my thinking about ethics, although this has taken a turn for which he is in no way responsible.

I have presented elements of this book to three academic audiences, all of which have done me good by asking tough questions—Wesleyan University, the University of Chicago, and the LBJ School of Public Affairs at the University of Texas at Austin. Even more valuable was a day's workshop with Ernesto Cortés' Industrial Areas Foundation, which gave me insight into how my issues affect working teams in the real world. I owe heartfelt thanks also to C. Cale McDowell for taking time from his busy career in law to write the afterword to this book. My editor Peter Ohlin and readers for the press made useful suggestions for revision. At a crucial stage, Ian Oliver read the manuscript and helped me improve it, Collin Bjork assisted me in the final editing, and Crystal Onyema polished the index.

Throughout the process of thinking and writing, Lucia Norton Woodruff has been a constant source of wisdom.

PART ONE

Introductory

| Ajax

Ajax is extraordinary in his size, in his strength, in his courage, and in the depth of his loyalty to the army, which he sees as a band of friends. He is the largest of the soldiers at Troy, he is the strongest, and he has saved the lives of more of his friends than anyone else over the period of this nine-year war. He has enjoyed the role he has played, but he expects to be honored for it. He is extraordinary in many ways, but we must not see anything unusual in his reaction to what he sees as an insult. He is like us, only bigger.

Ajax is not extraordinary in his hunger for honor and respect. We have all felt like Ajax on some dark day or night when we have not been treated with the respect we feel is due to us. And when we have lost out on honor, we may come to feel that we are no longer members of the community that we had formerly believed to be ours. The opposite of honor is insult, and insults drive people out.

In today's workplace, complaints about salaries and bonuses often have more to do with honor than they do with financial need. If you pay him more than you pay me, that shows you value him more, and that hurts my sense of honor—especially if, like Ajax, I have given you my all. In that case, I may take your decision about my salary as an insult. Insults lead to anger.

Ajax has a huge capacity for anger. But this too is not unusual. Honor and anger are wired to the same fuse. Nothing arouses anger so surely, or so fiercely, as an insult. Plato understood this when, in the *Republic*, he grounded both anger and honor in the same part of the soul (the *thumoeides*). Anger rises when honor is denied, and when anger rises, community breaks.

Other loyal soldiers, watching the case of Ajax, may come to question their own loyalty to the army. Do they really belong? Are their contributions recognized? If Ajax, who has done so much, is not rewarded, what hope do the rest of them have?

Full membership in a community depends on certain feelings, and these feelings are easily starved. A community is a circle of respect, and respect is felt. When any of us do not feel respected by the community, we withdraw. In a university, students who feel out of it hide out in their dorm rooms or simply go home. Faculty in a similar condition stop attending meetings, refuse committee assignments, and take on no extra work for the good of the whole. In an army, low-ranking soldiers, when they are disaffected, obey orders slowly or not at all and may actually take steps to sabotage their mission. These behaviors show up equally in the civilian workplace. But disaffection among armed soldiers can be lethal. In extreme cases, frightened soldiers would rather arrange to have their officers killed than follow them into danger. In all too many cases, troubled soldiers take their own lives. Suicide is the ultimate withdrawal, the sharpest expression of the idea that I have no place in this body of friends. They belong; I do not.

When the prize goes to Odysseus, Ajax realizes that, to Agamemnon, he has always been only a dumb ox, easily controlled. He sees that for all these years of warfare he has been used—taken advantage of, by men he used to believe were his friends. The Greek army, a band of friends who have been everything to him, is now palpably closed in a circle that leaves him outside. His sense of belonging, which had sustained him for nine years, has been an illusion from the start. Now at last he sees through that illusion.

Ajax is ignorant on an important point, however, and this ignorance fires his anger to the breaking point. Ajax does not understand the value of Odysseus's contributions. He despises people who depend on the power of words, and he has contempt for anyone who would win a battle by stealth. When Ajax dismisses the power of words and stratagems, he speaks for the dominant culture of ancient Greece. Actions are what matter, and they happen on the field of battle; words serve only to cloud judgment, and they do that in the camp, at night, or in meetings that waste the daylight. So Ajax thinks.

The line between action and words is never clear, however. At the end of his life, Ajax will find that he too has the power of words, now that he needs it. He never needed it before. But now that he does need words, he will talk himself brilliantly out of a tight situation. So don't pigeonhole Ajax as a dumb ox. He may be strong, but he is not stupid. Don't pigeonhole Odysseus either. He too will surprise us before the story is over. Still, the glory of Ajax has been in action, in the exercise of his strength, and the glory of Odysseus will be in deception.

Watching Agamemnon and the other Greeks succumb to Odysseus's power of words is deeply galling to Ajax. If he agrees to submit the decision to a panel of his peers, he would do so thinking they would be considering the facts. But as the process unfolds, he will start to feel that it is not about facts at all but about Odysseus's ability to bewitch a crowd with his words. That is why he will protest even before the speeches are done.

Ajax is wrong. Troy will not be won on the battlefield. It will be won, improbably, by the Trojan horse—which only an Odysseus could imagine.

The Children of Ajax

Ask yourself who is Ajax and who is Odysseus in any line of work today or in recent history. The categories are not exhaustive, but they include a great many people. No real person corresponds perfectly to the archetype of an Ajax or an Odysseus. Indeed, the characters in the myth are not as clearly different as we might expect. Ajax has brains, and Odysseus has brawn and courage. Still, these two categories are useful for sorting out issues of justice and rewards.

A modern Ajax who set an example for his profession was General Ulysses S. Grant—despite his first name. A poor student at the U. S. Military Academy, Grant was nevertheless a fine general, in the mode of Ajax. His military doctrine was simple: "Find out where your enemy is. Get at him as soon as you can. Strike him as hard as you can and as soon as you can, and keep moving on."[1] What this doctrine leaves unsaid is that Grant took the time to outnumber his enemy and make sure his troops had more ammunition than the enemy. Since Grant, U.S. infantry doctrine has followed the Ajax plan, to the detriment of our efforts in counterinsurgency operations in Vietnam and later.

Grant is a model of a modern Ajax in his use of words as well as in his military actions. He was always a man of few words who hated making speeches, even as a politician. Before the second day of Shiloh, General Sherman approached him with the intent to suggest retreat. "Well, Grant," he said, "we've had the devil's own day, haven't we." "Yes," said Grant. "Lick 'em tomorrow, though." And he did, using tactics admired by John Keegan—and a much augmented force.[2] But, as Ajax will do, at the end of his life, he produced plenty of words when he found that he needed them. Writing through pain, he brought off a best-selling memoir that he hoped would save his family from poverty after he died—as he knew he would—of cancer. In the end he did succeed through words, as he had through action, long before, on the field of battle.

Some wars call for an Ajax, others for an Odysseus. And even the same war may call for one and then the other, as the two sides seek new ways to win. The war in Vietnam called for an Odysseus to fight the insurgency, but it was given to an Ajax, General William Westmoreland.[3] Then, in 1973, when the army of South Vietnam had finally been prepared to contain insurgency, the United States withdrew and in 1974 cut support for the South Vietnamese army to the bone. Soon after that, in 1975, the North Vietnamese unleashed Ajax on the South in the form of armored columns, which the South Vietnamese had not been equipped to resist.[4]

The U.S. Army tends to promote Ajax, rarely Odysseus, to positions of power—Westmoreland in Vietnam, and a string of Ajaxes in Iraq until General David Petraeus was finally brought in.[5] Overseeing the ROTC program in my university, I have seen one fine Ajax after another sent to command the unit, and only one officer I would count as an Odysseus. In fact, the system is unjust for Odysseus, who will have a tough time reaching the rank of general. The U.S. Navy, by contrast, has honored the wily seaman for most of its history, from John Paul Jones through the brilliant plan at Midway and on down to our own day.[6]

The children of Ajax run through civilian life as well. Like Ajax, they are often asked to sacrifice honor in order to keep the peace, and many of them see no alternative but to do so. "No man would sacrifice his honor for the one he loves," exclaims Torvald, the naive husband, in Ibsen's *Doll's House*. "It is a thing hundreds of thousands of women have done," counters his wife, Nora.[7] Like Ajax, she has saved the life she thinks most important to her, the life of the man she loves. And, like Ajax, she will pull away when she sees that her contribution is not valued. But unlike Ajax, she chooses to live, to carve out independence through education. This woman is not content to be a daughter of Ajax, and she has the power to escape the Ajax role. Few of Ajax's daughters are so lucky.[8]

Most versions of the ancient story presuppose that Ajax should have won the armor. The version I follow leaves the question open but suggests that Odysseus was the rightful winner. Whether or not Odysseus should have won, justice fails Ajax. Justice, as we shall see, is not merely getting the right outcome. True justice must resolve a conflict in a way that leaves the community whole; this decision leaves the Greek army in a ruptured state that could have been fatal to it. In this case, a decision for the right outcome turned out wrong. It's not merely *what* you decide that matters, but *how* you decide it, and how you communicate the decision.

Notes

1. Quoted in Keegan (1987), p. 194. Much has been written about Grant and his way of making war, but Keegan's astute observations are a good place to begin.

2. On the episode, and its aftermath, see Keegan (1987), p. 168, p. 225, and following.

3. By mid-1967, the United States had 450,000 troops in Vietnam, and Westmoreland was asking for 200,000 more. But the huge blows his large force was able to land on the enemy were like the effect of "a sledgehammer on a floating cork" (Malcolm Brown, quoted in Herring [1979], p. 156).

4. Herring (1979), p. 258; Lawrence (2008), pp. 102–108.

5. In an influential paper in *Armed Forces Journal,* Lieutenant Colonel Paul Yingling (2007) writes: "It is unreasonable to expect that an officer who spends 25 years conforming to institutional expectations will emerge as an innovator in his late forties....To improve the creative intelligence of our generals, Congress must change the officer promotion system in ways that reward adaptation and intellectual achievement."

6. At Midway, the Japanese naval force, which aimed to ambush the U.S. Navy, was itself caught in an ambush.

7. Henrik Ibsen, *A Doll's House,* in *Four Great Plays by Henrik Ibsen*, translated by R. Farquharson Sharp (Toronto and New York: Bantam, 1958).

8. Women who are children of Ajax may be in an especially weak position. They may be trained by their cultures to set less store by honor and to be less free with their anger, than the original Ajax. This would be to the advantage of the Agamemnons in their lives, who would tend to exploit their willingness to set aside their honor. I owe the point to Elise Springer of Wesleyan University.

What Is at Stake: Rewards versus Booty and Incentives

> Employees were particularly outraged that even as the company fell into bankruptcy, top managers awarded themselves $57.3 million in court-approved bonuses while 4,200 people lost their jobs and the workers who remained went without raises.
>
> —*New York Times,* October 23, 2010, B7,
> on the Tribune Company

Booty is a share of a community's profits; its opposite is a share of the losses. An incentive is a management tool for influencing behavior; its opposite is a penalty. A bonus or reward recognizes success and confers honor. One treasure can serve in all three capacities, as booty, incentive, and reward, but the three conceptions are different. The opposite of honor is insult; sometimes, as in the case reported above by the New York Times, and in the case of Ajax, a distribution of rewards is an insult to those passed over.

A special feature of the reward/insult pair is that they rub off on groups. If Ajax is insulted by Odysseus, all the foot soldiers feel hurt; if he is honored, their morale improves because they see him as one of them. This factor is especially important in communities that are divided by race or gender.

By "reward" in these pages I mean a gift that singles you out as an individual (but which may indirectly honor your group). Among the most spectacular rewards in modern history was the gift of Blenheim Palace to the Duke of Marlborough. The British nation gave it to him in gratitude for his great victory.[1]

Achilles' armor is a reward. So is an individual bonus, a merit raise, or a promotion based on merit. Selection for high office in a political community is also a reward. A reward is any good thing given by a community to one of its members in recognition of what that person in particular has done. Rewards give honor to those who receive them. Honor is a basic human need, which any healthy community supplies.

So why not honor everyone by giving everyone a reward? That would be like an elementary school field day in which every child is given a gold medal. Worthless from the point of view of honor. If goodies are handed out indiscriminately, they carry no honor. There is nothing special about being treated like everyone else. Stock or stock options for all employees are not rewards. Promotions based on time in grade are not rewards. Policies that try to make everyone happy will make no one happy in the arena of honor. A reward (in the sense I am using in this book) recognizes what you, and only you, have done.

When Agamemnon's army takes Troy, they will divide the booty—the treasure, the women, and the slaves—among themselves. Each will receive a share that is proportional to his position in the army. The British navy gave out prize money in a similar fashion 200 years ago. We would call such payments piracy or theft if they were not traditional incentives to win at war. These payments were usually contractual, rather like the shares claimed by successful plaintiffs' lawyers. Contractual payments are not rewards. They carry no special honor.

If, however, an individual is deprived of a share of the loot, that would bring great dishonor. That is why, in Book 1 of the *Iliad*, Agamemnon felt he had to take Achilles' woman away from him when Achilles insisted that Agamemnon return a girl—part of Agamemnon's booty—to her father. As king, Agamemnon felt great pressure to sustain his honor. So he took Achilles' booty for his own. Naturally, Achilles went into a sulk, because his share had been diminished in violation of the contract. Losing his share of the booty was a terrible insult to Achilles. Such deprivations affect honor because they single out individuals.

We could all benefit equally from the same incentives (as in the case of booty or stock options), but we could not all benefit equally from rewards or other honors. Incentives do not necessarily recognize anyone as an individual; that is why they carry no honor— unless they are doubling as rewards. Sometimes a reward is an incentive. This is especially true for promotions and merit raises. People who know what they need to do to win a promotion or a raise may well do that precisely to win the reward.

So a reward may be an incentive, but not all incentives are rewards. When the criteria for rewards are transparent and the decision procedures are public, then the rewards are incentives for members to meet the published criteria. And then the system of rewards is most in accordance with fairness. Indeed, employees often ask for this sort of fairness in reward systems. Some academic departments treat merit raises in this way—so much merit increase in salary for a book with a major publisher, so much for an article in one of the journals listed as highly ranked.

Suppose Agamemnon offers this to the army: the soldier who kills the most Trojans with his own weapons in the next ten days will win the armor. Then the armor serves as both reward and incentive. Agamemnon is wise not to take this option, for two reasons. The first is that this would bias the contest toward Ajax, who clearly has more killing power than Odysseus. And that seems unjust. The second drawback is that this would not help win the war. Troy will not be defeated by attrition, as the city has many allies sending troops from the hills. Rewarding a body count will lead to a lot of killing, but the people who are now dead may not have been a serious threat to a Greek victory. They may not even be Trojans.[2]

Suppose, on the other hand, Agamemnon proposes to give the armor to the soldier with the best stratagem for victory. Odysseus could win that hands down with a proposal to build the Trojan Horse. Here we encounter two similar drawbacks. This offer would unjustly spin the reward against Ajax. To make matters worse, fairness would require that the Trojan Horse proposal be evaluated in public by a panel of neutral experts. But that would reward a dead horse. Trojan Horses, to stay alive, must be well-kept secrets.

Rewards that are also incentives appeal the most to hard-working Ajaxes, who can gear up to do what they are asked. Such rewards offer the least to innovators such as Odysseus. That is because incentives depend for their effect on criteria stated in advance, but an Odysseus may invent a strategy so new that it could not meet any criteria that management would know enough to lay out ahead of time.

In much of life, as in the Trojan War, no one knows enough to identify the criteria that will produce the most valuable behavior. More than one financial business has ruined itself by offering powerful incentives to executives to take steps that raise share-holder equity over the short term. The criteria were clear enough, but the connection between them and the survival of the company was not.

Not all incentives are rewards, and not all rewards are incentives. In the arena where they overlap, where rewards are incentives, fairness tends to destroy justice and undermine long-term goals (see "The Fairness Trap" later in the book). Fair and transparent incentives may be effective management, but managing people is not the same as leading them. Leadership requires justice. To achieve justice, leadership often has to give up on fairness.

Incentives and penalties are management tools. Incentives and penalties do not belong to the language of leadership. Good people will follow a great leader whether booty is in the picture or not. If you are in charge, and you cannot influence people in your group except by means of incentives and penalties, you have not served as a leader.

Problems about incentives can be solved by following good management practices. But the Ajax dilemma is about rewards, and it cannot be solved. That is why I call it a dilemma. Dilemmas call for leadership, something that is famously missing from the Greek army. It is missing from many communities. Sad to say, dilemmas are common, but leadership is rare.

Leadership as I understand it is an ethical concept, a matter of good character. I know that many people use the word as nearly synonymous with management, which can be good or bad, ethical or unethical. But in my usage, leadership cannot be rated as good or bad. In this it is like justice itself. We don't need to speak of good justice, because we cannot speak of bad justice: if it is not good it is not justice. Similarly, it would be redundant to say that certain leaders are good; of course they are good; their influence as leaders depends on their goodness. We should not say that a leader is bad; we should say, instead, that this person has failed to be a leader.

Notes

1. See Lucas (1980), pp. 188–189.
2. The body count as a measure of success was not successful as used by the U.S. forces in Vietnam in the late 1960s because, although many Vietnamese people were killed in the campaign, the enemy could withstand far more serious attrition. At the same time, since not all of those killed were actually with the enemy, the policy alienated many civilians. Moreover, such an incentive policy distracted U.S. forces from the smarter tactics that could have been more effective, and have been effective in other counterinsurgencies. On the issue see, for example, Herring (1979), pp. 153–156.

PART TWO

The Story of Ajax

"I saved your life by the ships," said Ajax, pointing at Agamemnon. "And yours, and yours. And you over there—you hid behind me in the battle by the wall. You two, do you remember? You both hid behind my shield. I even saved his life (pointing to Odysseus). Has anyone done more for you? I rest my case. The armor is mine."

The scene is Troy, a city in Asia Minor near the shore of the Hellespont. The time is before history, the time of myth. Our story is one episode in a tale of epic proportions—the war of the Greek army against the Trojans. The Greeks are camped by their ships along the shore, while the Trojans are at home in their walled city.

After nine years of war the Greek army is still determined to take Troy. Both sides have sustained heavy losses; both sides continue to receive reinforcements. Achilles has killed Hector, the best fighter in Troy. Achilles has been the great hope of the Greeks, but now he too is dead, shot through the heel, the only place he can be hurt. His armor is to be a prize for the finest soldier in the Greek army. A trophy beyond price, this armor is spectacular. The god Hephaestus made it of precious metals in his workshop on Olympus.

Two candidates come forward, Ajax and Odysseus. Each makes a strong claim for the armor. But there is only one prize. Only one soldier can be the finest, the most valuable. And Achilles had just one suit of armor. So a decision must be made.

To pick the winner, the Greek commander convenes a panel of soldiers, choosing them by a lottery, like a modern jury.

Ajax is best in all the qualities expected of a soldier. He is the biggest, the strongest, the bravest, and the most loyal. He is also a good basic tactician; he knows where he is needed on the battle-field and always manages to be there. He has saved the lives of many of his comrades. He is huge, and his shield is more huge; men shelter behind him the way today's troops shelter behind a tank.

Odysseus has the best command of words. He is no slouch on the field of battle, but he is a champion in the use of words. And he is devious. He is a man of many wiles. He can lie himself out of almost any situation. He has been inside the citadel of Troy and come out safely. We know that he will devise the famous horse that will deceive the Trojans, and even now the Trojans know that only Odysseus can defeat them. Their walls will hold out against anything but deception.

The two candidates speak before the panel, and each makes his case. After that, there is no contest. Odysseus is the better speaker by far. In any case, the Greeks know what the Trojans know: Troy can survive any conventional attack by the Greeks. No matter how hard they work, no matter how brave they are, the Greeks will never bring Troy down by the methods they have been using so far. Only Odysseus can provide them with the winning edge. And so the panel votes unanimously to give the prize to Odysseus.

Ajax is astonished and angry. He is sure that he has been robbed: the highest honor was plainly due to him. The jury must have been bribed. Or else they were tricked by Odysseus. One way or another, Ajax is sure, he has been betrayed by Agamemnon and the army he used to love.

Ajax goes berserk.

From this point, let the other participants tell the story as I imagine it. Is there anything they could have done to prevent the loss of Ajax?

Odysseus Looks Back

He tried to kill me this morning. I wept for him then. This afternoon, I saved him from a punishment worse than death. At sunset, his family buried him, with my help, and I wept for him again for the last time. He does not need my friendship any longer. He is safe, and he is a hero.

When I think of my friend Ajax, even now, I think of his big heart, his loyalty, and his kindness to his friends. I believe that our friendship could have survived—it did survive, after all, in my mind, and I am the survivor of the two of us. I also believe that he could have lived—but in another army, an army very different from the one we know. I keep asking myself what that army would be like. What I want is an army where our friendship could go on forever, or at least for as long as we lived. That would be the army for us. But there was no army like that in the world Ajax inhabited. I dream there will be such an army in mine. This army of ours made us enemies. Our army should never have done that to us.

Ajax changed my mind about him, a few years ago. It happened when I was chosen to talk Achilles out of his anger. You know the story: Achilles had been treated badly by Agamemnon, who took away his trophy girl out of spite. Then Achilles went into a sulk and planned to take his troops and go home. But we needed him to stay and fight. Agamemnon and the others picked me to be their spokesman. My mission was to talk Achilles into staying with us. They chose me because no one else had a gift for persuasion equal to mine. I can do just about anything with words. I can even tell the truth, as I am now. But don't expect me to do that very often.

So I went to Achilles. A few other good speakers came to back me up. We felt we absolutely had to succeed. None of us could imagine victory without Achilles. Time after time he had turned the tide of battle. He could move around the field like the wind, "swift-footed Achilles." He could always be where we needed him. But after he got the sulks, we had been losing and losing and losing. And we were afraid that if he went home, we'd never get him back. That is why we were sent to him. If we could persuade him to stay on, we were pretty sure he'd take pity on us and come back into the field.

Ajax tagged along because he was the one who had been hurt the most by Achilles' decision to divorce himself from the army. Ajax had no other real family—other than the army, I mean. His situation back home was precarious. True, he had a woman in the camp; he called her his wife, and he had a son by her. He also had an illegitimate half brother. We in the army treated his woman and child and brother as if they were a real family to him, but that would not have happened back home. His true family was the army, as everyone knew; so if Achilles left us, Ajax's family would be broken.

That is how a group of us went to Achilles. I spoke first. I was as eloquent as the sirens who sing in the sea. I told him what Agamemnon promised to do for him if he stayed. It was a magnificent offer. But Achilles looked dead at me and said, "I hate like the gates of hell a man who says one thing and holds another in his heart." I don't know what he meant by that. I believed what I said that day. Maybe he thought Agamemnon was lying. Or maybe he thought that I was so tricky with words he could never believe me about anything.

Others spoke, to no effect, and we were about to turn and go home. But the feelings had been building up in Ajax like spoiled meat many days after a barbecue. They had to come vomiting out, no matter what. He was angry and grieving. He used few words, just enough to remind Achilles that they were friends, that they had a long history of depending on each other, of helping each other out. And Achilles stayed. Because of Ajax, he stayed. He didn't go back into the field—yet—but he stayed in the camp. That is how I learned about Ajax's power with words; he had it when he needed it. He needed it this morning, and from what I heard, he found a spectacular fountain of words.

So I changed my mind about Ajax. I used to think he was a friendly, loyal, bighearted lunk who had muscles where other people kept their intelligence. I now saw that this was not so. He had never needed many words, because he could pack such strong feelings into the words he used. I had thought he was a man of few words because he was stupid, or because he could get his way by force. But I was wrong.

I loved him. We were friends. Ajax was more than twice my size, and I am not a small man. His shield was even bigger than he was; no one else could carry it. When things got bad, two or three of us would take shelter behind him, and none of the Trojans dared to go after us. He was always there, where the danger was greatest. He never complained about hard work. If we had a prize for strength or size or loyalty or even bravery, Ajax would win it. But this prize was for the most valuable soldier. Ask any Trojan and you'll get the same answer:

"The Greek soldier who frightens us most is Odysseus. He's the one with brains. You never know where he'll turn up or what he'll do next. He'll capture a Trojan at night, sweet-talk him into letting out all our secrets, and then kill him without a second thought. He'll sneak into our citadel and steal a sacred statue. If Troy ever falls to the Greeks, there's only one way it will happen. Troy is too strong to be defeated by brute force. That wily Odysseus will come up with some trick or other. That's what we fear. That's why Odysseus is the only one who really scares us. Ajax? Oh, he terrifies us, of course, when he's near us in battle. But we can see him a mile away, and there's only one of him. Odysseus is all over the battle-field; his clever stratagems double the effectiveness of every other Greek soldier."

That's what the Trojans will say, any of them. Believe me, I have taken prisoners, while I was in disguise, and I have asked them what they fear. Everyone knows this, and that is why I won the prize. The simple fact is that I am the most valuable soldier in the army. The panel they chose by lot came to that conclusion. Any panel would have done the same. What could be more fair than that? Ajax made his case, and I made mine. It was brains against brawn and brains won. Brains always win in the end. So they awarded the armor to me. Fair is fair.

But Ajax felt strongly in his heart that he should have been the winner, and so he felt the same way that the Trojans did about us Greeks. The Trojans thought they'd never be beaten except by some clever ruse. Ajax felt that the only way I could have beaten him was by playing a trick. And of course I did make a brilliant speech, if I do say so. Most of it was true. But all of it was convincing. Ajax made a speech too. But all he could say was, "I saved your life, didn't I?" to one or another man on the panel. But that was the wrong question. Ajax lost.

Then he lost his mind. He tried to kill me along with the other commanders. I understand that. Any old soldier knows how easy it is to go over the edge. We live with violence every day. We fight for the sake of honor. We live for the sake of honor. Take honor away from a man like Achilles or Ajax and you had better expect the human equivalent of a major earthquake. Ajax in his rage—that could have been me. I pitied him.

Now it is over. It started yesterday, with the contest.

Agamemnon Arranges the Contest

I am a good king. Ajax has no place in my army. He should have accepted my decision without a murmur. But he's too pigheaded. Or, I should say, he is too ox-headed. He wouldn't understand justice if it was sitting in front of him as big as a lion. I did everything right, but he just can't seem to see that.

If I had made the decision on my own, in private, no one would accept it, either way. Both of these men are my friends. Either way I decided, the loser would accuse me of being a better friend to the other one. So I did the right thing. I followed an ancient tradition of our people and convened a panel of jurors from the army, chosen by lot. I did it quickly, leaving no time for either party to bribe the panel once it had been selected. I did not allow any close friend of either candidate to be included in the lottery. I did all this in the clear light of day in front of the assembled army. Everyone saw that this was fair. Their friends on both sides sat apart, the others drew lots, the panel was formed. Immediately, before anyone could bribe them or threaten them, the men who were chosen sat in judgment.

So none of this is my fault. I did everything right. I put the burden on the panel. I charged them to make a decision and report it to me. I went further. I wanted to make sure that no argument on either side was left out of consideration. So I invited each side to present its arguments, and I gave each side an opportunity to rebut the other. I gave both sides equal time for speech and rebuttal, measured by the best means we have to measure time—a device that drips water out at the same rate no matter what. Same amount of water, same amount of time. And so it was.

Ajax and Odysseus drew lots to see who would speak first, and Ajax won. He was not eloquent, but he had a strong case, using only half his time. The army listened in silence and then applauded. After that, Odysseus spoke and made his case. He was eloquent, but he hardly needed to be, his case was so strong. Then it was time for rebuttal.

That's when I saw trouble ahead. Ajax was seething with rage when he stood to give his rebuttal. He could not believe that anyone would listen to an argument against him. He pleaded with the panel. He stormed at them. He stormed at me. The decision had not been made, but he hated everything about the way we were making it. "You call this justice?" he bellowed. "You think it's OK to give equal time to that charlatan, that liar, that pint-sized bag-of-tricks? Why should he have any time at all? You all know me. You all know him. I told you the truth about what I had done to save your lives in battle. You must not listen to his rebuttal. You know he has no case; you know he's wrong. Shout him down. I have earned the armor many times over with my sweat and blood. All he has ever done is sneak around and talk smooth. Do not let him say another word. I hold you all to be my friends. I would save the life of any one of you. Do the same for me. My honor is at stake, and that means a lot more to me than my life. Save my honor, save me. Give me the prize. Above all, do not insult me by listening to a word this man says."

This time there was no applause. They listened in silence. Ajax stopped again before the water ran out; he did not have much more to say. Odysseus rose and spoke calm words, beautiful words. He praised Ajax. "This wonderful man!" he said. "You know how great he is. But just now you have seen his limitations. He simply does not understand how justice is done. All he understands is his own muscle power and loyalty to his friends. You know that those two things—muscle power and loyalty—will never bring down the towers of Troy. Only strategy will do that, and we will need a very clever strategy at that. I can't say in public what I will do. It has to be a secret. But you can be sure that Ajax will never win this war. At least I have the tools to do the job, if you follow my advice."

The panel conferred briefly and then their spokesman came to me. He whispered in my ear: the panel had been unanimous. The prize went to Odysseus. But they were afraid to say this out loud. They saw that Ajax was on the edge of losing control; they were afraid he would turn violent.

That crazy lummox! Who could have known in advance that he cared so much about his honor? What did he need honor for? We all knew he was the biggest. Any idiot could see that. And loyal? I never knew a man who cared so much about his friends. When any one of us was in trouble, there he would be, surging through a wave of our enemies, pushing that huge shield in front of him like the prow of a cargo ship.

I am not the least bit sorry that he lost. What good is a soldier who can't take orders? Yes, he was big and strong and loyal to his friends. But an army is not a bunch of friends. It has to have discipline. An army is an orderly, disciplined assembly of troops working to achieve their mission under a unified command. That is where I come in: I am the commander; the other kings here are bound by oath to follow my commands. Not by friendship. By oath. They swore to obey me. That is what makes this an army, rather than a rabble with weapons.

All those great things Ajax did—not one of them did he do because I gave an order to him to do it. He never waited for orders. He saw what needed to be done on the battlefield and waded right in to do it. He fought because of the love he had for his friends. That's all. All about friends. But my army does not need friends, and neither do I as commander. I have an army of soldiers, and they are all sworn to obey.

An army needs unified command as much as a community needs justice. When all is said and done, in an army, the soldiers need to obey the commander, with justice or without it. But Ajax was his own man. I could see that I would lose his friendship the moment I ordered the armor to be taken to Odysseus's shelter.

That big ox was too dumb to understand what it means to be bound by an oath. All he knew was friendship. And his idea of friendship was so simple-minded: He would save the lives of his friends, and, in return, they would admire him for his strength. That was it. That was all there was to Ajax.

But I am getting ahead of myself. The army waited in silence for the verdict. I agreed with the spokesman; it was not safe to announce the verdict as things were at the time. I asked Nestor what to do next. Nestor is the oldest among the kings who serve here under my command, and he is by far the wisest.

So I asked: Should I have Ajax arrested before the verdict came out? Lock him up to avoid violence? What could I do to keep the army whole? Wouldn't he agree that the decision is just? Odysseus is plainly the more valuable soldier. But a lot of people will want me to keep Ajax in the army at all costs. Are they as wrong as I think they are? Should I pay attention to them?

Nestor was old and wise. Somehow, he said, we would have to win Ajax over. He advised me to declare a mistrial and start over. I did. I told the army that this matter was very important for our future. We could make no quick decision. I declared a mistrial.

Ajax was furious. He said he would sit outside his shelter and wait for us to bring him the armor. "I will give you till dawn," he said. "Talk all night if you like that sort of thing. It doesn't matter to me. But at dawn I expect you to deliver the armor."

I asked what he meant: "Is that a threat?"

"I tell only the truth," Ajax answered. "I expect you to give me what I deserve. You are right to call this a mistrial; it has been ruined by that bag-of-tricks. Don't say you need more time. You are king. You have the authority to set things straight this instant. Every moment you delay is another insult to me."

I answered: "I am king and not a tyrant. I need time to consult the elders. But I promise you, let Zeus be my witness, I will give you what you deserve," I said. "No less and no more. Be patient."

He turned his back on me and walked away. The army dispersed in silence.

After the Contest: Tecmessa's Night Visit to the Generals

I was terrified when my husband came home and sat outside staring back at the line of ships that led away toward Agamemnon's shelter. He would not eat or drink. I had heard the gossip. Don't think we don't know what the men are doing. We are in every shelter, and we talk to each other. He had made a threat against the high king, and the whole army had heard it. I knew he meant it. Ajax never said a thing he did not mean in his whole life. I knew this would end in tears, for me and my child and everyone else, unless the king took pity on us.

When it was dark I slipped out, wearing a dark cloak, and crept down the line to the king's shelter. It was much bigger than any of the others, because they had meetings inside, for the generals. Between the front wall and the side of his ship they had slung a sail to shade the entrance and provide a place for people to wait when they had business with the king. I heard voices inside. Agamemnon's was firm, Odysseus's calm, Menelaus's angry. Nestor's old broken voice had a higher pitch: "We are talking in circles," he said. "Like men lost in the woods on a dark night with no stars to guide them. Why don't you listen, now, to an old man?"

I was determined to enter and to be heard. Women are supposed to be seen only, and never heard except at funerals when they are permitted to mourn aloud. But I had no man to speak for me. Ajax was crazy. My son was only six years old. My brother-in-law was hunting in the hills. There was only me to save my husband and my family. I would do anything. I had brought gold to bribe the guard, but it did not work. So I started to shout and chant, "I want to speak with the king."

Odysseus came. I told him I would go on shouting until I was told I could speak with the king. He said, "You and your husband are quite a pair." But he said it kindly. "You may be able to help us out of our dilemma. I'll see what I can do." Soon he was back. "You may enter," he said, "but on certain conditions. You must not speak until the king asks you to do so. You must address him as 'Lord of Men.' When he is finished with you, you must leave in silence. He hates to hear a woman scream. Do you promise all that?" I did. "You have friends inside," he went on. And from his voice I knew Odysseus was a man who liked women, who would listen to a woman.

Inside, the four men sat around a small table, Agamemnon, his brother Menelaus, the old counselor Nestor, and Odysseus. I had never seen Odysseus so close before. I had expected him to be a shrimp of a man, someone who made up in cleverness what he was missing in muscle. But the dim lamplight showed me an athlete in early middle age, tougher looking than the kings. Agamemnon was called the lord of men, but he was not the lord of me or of any woman, from what I hear about his wife. He was red-faced, paunchy, starting to lose hair. Menelaus looked pretty much the same, but a few years younger. We all knew he could not keep a woman. Nestor had white hair and a white beard, neatly trimmed.

Agamemnon gazed at my breasts, which are rather full, and scratched his chin. "You look like just the thing we need. They say that Persuasion is the daughter of Aphrodite. Put that another way: sex is the mother of persuasion. That's for sure. We were just asking ourselves who might persuade Ajax to accept our judgment. And no one came to mind. Our best speakers would be wasted on Ajax. He has no respect for intelligence. But you might just do the trick. They say that a small whip moves a big ox, but your big breasts might do it even better."

Nestor intervened. "There's no need to be insulting."

He was right. I was insulted. I had been a princess in my own land before the Greeks destroyed it and led me out, past the corpses of my brothers and my father, leaving behind the plume of smoke that was my city rising to the sky. We Phrygians have always been better educated than Greeks, and I was the most talented woman of my age group. I could sing great poems, I could play the lyre, I could dance with the cream of the maidens to celebrate the goddess in the spring. I opened my mouth and started to speak. Odysseus pinched my arm and I stopped.

"No, no," said Agamemnon. "Surely she knows a compliment when she hears it." He turned to me again: "As I was saying, I want you to use all your charms to calm the anger in Ajax's breast. We are afraid that he will do something foolish. If you can just hold him off till his anger subsides, maybe everything will be all right. Will you do this for us? You have permission to speak."

"Lord of men, Agamemnon, you are wise to consider the anger of Ajax. I am terribly afraid. If we are not careful, he will go out of his mind. I have no fear for you; you are well protected by your guards and your own strength." ("Flatter them," I said to myself. "Make them feel strong and wise.") "What I fear is that he will go crazy and attack you in public. Then you will have to move against him, and we will all be the worse for it. You will lose your strongest and bravest soldier. I know he is not your best; I have asked both men and women, and all agree. It is Odysseus who deserves the prize. But you absolutely need Ajax. What good are brains, if you don't have the muscles to carry out their plans?"

The old man, Nestor, spoke up in his reedy voice. "You understand the situation precisely. I thought we could rely on you."

"But you can't," I said. "He sits outside our shelter staring this way. He will not move, he will not speak. I have used all my powers. I prayed to the sex-goddess Aphrodite, but she did not hear me. Ajax would not allow me to touch his body. I brought him our son. He brushed the little boy aside. The boy cried. It made no difference. There is no more I can do. But there is one thing you can do. That is why I came to you."

"Go on," said Odysseus.

"Give him the armor. I know he does not deserve it, but that is the only way to save him. And you must save him to save the army."

"We thought of that. I won't do it," said Agamemnon. "I am *basileus*. You're not Greek so you won't know what that means. It means I am both king and judge. It means I must serve justice. I will never give any man a thing I know he does not deserve."

Odysseus interrupted: "But you are also a military commander. You must serve your mission, which is to keep the army together until we have won Troy. Tecmessa, please tell us why you think we should give him the armor. I see you have more to say."

"It is the only way to save Ajax's life. You must either kill him or give him the armor. The choice is simple. For the sake of the army."

Agamemnon exploded. "For the sake of the army? They will never trust me again if I do not do what is right. You talk like a woman."

Then Odysseus after a brief silence: "Am I a woman? I will say the same thing she does. Send him the armor. She talks like a human being, and so do I. You or I or anyone could fall into a blind rage like the one that has made Ajax so helpless and so beyond help. Yes, I have seen you when the god of blind rage danced on your head and you drove Achilles into a fit of sulks that almost cost us the whole war. And, yes, you may see me also, if I go back to Ithaca and find that some stay-at-home has been after my wife, you'd better believe I would lose control of myself. Maybe Nestor is too old for such passions, but the rest of us are not. Think what it is to be human. Show some compassion. I am already beginning to feel pity for Ajax. He has given his all for the army, and he is not bright enough to understand why that is not enough to win him the prize. Look at that armor! It is far too small for him. I know it is too large for me. In a week or two this will not matter to anyone. It is just a trophy. All it means is honor. And I do not need honor. For god's sake, Agamemnon, give him the armor and let's be done with this nightmare."

"This nightmare is of Ajax's making." Agamemnon was angry. "He's the one who fights against justice. If he flies off the handle, that's his fault. Not mine or anyone else's. And no one else but he should suffer for his fault. That's justice. While I am king, justice shall rule."

I had known all along we should never talk to Agamemnon about compassion. He has no more capacity for pity or self-understanding than a god on Olympus. But I had no other plea to make, and I felt I had to support Odysseus. So I knelt and grasped his knee in the manner of a suppliant. "Agamemnon, think of Ajax, whom you loved as a friend. Think of his son. Think of me. If Ajax dies, his son and I will be lost. We will have no one to protect us. Please!" I had tried reason, and that had not worked. Now was the time for tears. I burst into loud sobs and clung to his knee as he tried to move away from me.

I never thought this would move Agamemnon, but it might move the others, and they had some influence. I said the things I had heard from the poets, trying to put all my feeling into it: "You're a great king. You know you're not a god. Leave justice to the gods, leave it to Zeus. Zeus will do justice, he will always do justice, he always has. We are human. We all die like grass in summer, we fall like leaves in winter. Compassion is a sign of weakness. Yes, I understand that. But we are weak, even kings are weak. Please I beg you for your own sake, for the humanity you share with Ajax, for the humanity you share with me..." Pretty good lines, I thought.

Agamemnon spoke to Odysseus, interrupting. "We have listened to her, as you asked. It turns out that she will not help us. Now it is time for you to escort her safely back to Ajax." Then to me. "We will decide before the sun rises what to do."

Nestor Calls for a New Contest

I loved Ajax. Not for his strength and size, though the god knows he had those. I loved him for his big heart. And the moment Tecmessa entered, I fell in love with her too. I'm an old foolish man, and I would have done anything she asked, once I looked into her eyes. She was simply stunning. When Odysseus asked to bring her inside, Agamemnon asked, "Is she sexy?" And Odysseus said she was. But sexy isn't half of it. She was as strong as Ajax, but in a woman's way. Her eyes, the way she stood, her voice. The eyes were dark—surprising, really, in a woman with light blond hair.

I never would have expected a woman to speak so well. She did just what I would have advised, very cunning. When you plead for pity with a tough guy like Agamemnon, never use the word. Show him where his own self-interest lies, tell him you're just helping him to what is in his own interests. You don't have to say, "Be selfish," but you can show him that your proposal will make him more powerful. If you mention compassion at all, do so in order to condemn it. Then Odysseus made his appalling blunder. Compassion! What foolishness to bring to a lord of men like Agamemnon! I would have my work cut out for me to clean up the mess Odysseus made when he used that word.

Now do not misunderstand what I am about to say. I have the greatest respect for Agamemnon. A good king calls for advice before trouble breaks out, and Agamemnon had the good sense to call a council before reporting the verdict of our panel of jurors. But he showed appallingly bad judgment in setting up the contest in the way he did. Well, I admit he was following Greek custom—we always set aside a panel of jurors and have both sides make speeches, and then let the panel decide. That's how we do things. But why could Agamemnon not see that this was like setting a footrace to determine whether a runner or a spear thrower is the better athlete? It's worthless. A contest of speeches between a speechifier and a muscleman proves nothing.

No one disagrees with the outcome, no one but Ajax. Even Tecmessa knows who the winner should be. Agamemnon says he is committed to justice. But he has no idea what justice is. He thinks—this royal simpleton—that if the case comes out right, that's justice. But that is only half of it. We must have justice in the procedure as well as in the result.

So I asked Agamemnon to declare a mistrial. The procedure with the panel was plainly unjust. We would propose a new procedure and make sure that Ajax thought it was fair before we went any further. My suggestion was to capture a sample of Trojan soldiers next day, and ask them which of the two struck greater fear into their hearts.

Odysseus said, "Fair enough. But your prisoners will say the same thing. And it won't make Ajax feel any better to have Trojan prisoners corroborate the decision of the panel. He will lose more face, feel more insulted, be more angry." As I look back, I believe

Odysseus was right. But Agamemnon agreed that we should make the attempt. No one had a better idea.

Ajax was sitting in front of his shelter, staring my way as I came up to him. He said, "You don't have my armor. Dawn's coming." I replied, "Agamemnon changed his mind. He admits he was wrong to set up that panel. He would like to set up a new procedure for making the decision about the armor, with your agreement." He said nothing. I said, "If the procedure is fair enough, then, either you will win the armor, or Odysseus will. But either way, all of us will agree that justice has been done."

Ajax said nothing for a moment. Then again, "Dawn's coming."

Tecmessa Appeals to Love

Love is the only thing that will do the trick. Nothing but love is strong enough to stand up to a man's sense of honor. For love of his friend Patroclus, Achilles forgot the insult he'd been given by the king. It was for love that he went back to war. Well, of course, he did it to honor the man he loved, so honor was part of the story. Love of a woman is not so strong in this man's army. We women have learned that too often.

All this anger about the armor—it was really about honor. It was only about honor. There was nothing mercenary in my husband. Aside from the honor it carried, that suit of armor had no value. No one could melt it down for the precious metals, because, after all, it was made by a god, and it had been worn by Achilles. Ajax was too big to wear it, and Odysseus was too small. This fight was not about a suit of armor or the price of a suit of armor. It was about honor. The men in this army are mad about honor. Women like me lost their honor long ago. Honor means nothing to me. But I understand what it means to a man like Ajax. He was loyal because of his honor, brave because of his honor; everything he was he was because of his honor. And these fools canceled that out. They canceled him out.

Nestor said he could talk justice to Ajax and that would make him forget his honor. Nestor is a wise old man, but doesn't he see what men are like in this Greek army? They are all fools for honor, and so are the Trojans. My only hope for men is that they can be greater fools for love. Of course I could not expect a man to love a woman the way Achilles loved Patroclus. That would be impossible for a soldier, I think. And I am a spear-bride, after all. I was his share of the spoils after the Greeks took my town and destroyed it. I like to think he grew to like me, that he cares about me, but I know he did not take me out of love. I do know he loves his son. Maybe that will do the trick.

After my failure with Agamemnon, I returned to Ajax and tried to speak to him about his son. About his brother. About his soldiers, all these men who depend on him. I know he loved his soldiers. And I even begged him to think about me. As a spear-bride I would be lost if he died. But love was not strong enough. He sat on in silence.

Nestor came before dawn to talk to Ajax. Ajax listened quietly till Nestor had laid out his offer to do the whole contest over again, using a procedure that Ajax agreed to. Then he said his two words, "Dawn's coming."

Here's what I think Ajax had going in his head. "Tell Agamemnon I don't give a damn what method he uses for deciding.

He's the king, and he owes me the prize. What I saw today was disgusting: the king pretending to listen to that debate. Debate does not count for anything in an army. I'm no fool. Agamemnon is king. He wanted to give the prize to his buddy Odysseus all along, and that thing you call his 'procedure' just let him push the blame onto someone else. He's a coward. I don't care how he does it or who he blames when it's all over, but tell him to send me the armor before sunup." That was what was in his heart when he said those two words, "Dawn's coming."

"But if you agree to a new procedure, then it will be entirely fair...," Nestor started in again. Ajax said nothing.

I caught up with Nestor partway back to Agamemnon's. "Bring him the armor," I said. "Can't you see what's at stake here? His honor is on the line. He has given and given and given, of himself, for the army, day after day. How can you shame him like this?"

Nestor said, "There's no shame in losing a fair contest, no shame in being runner-up for the top prize. He needs to learn that, or he has no place in a civilized army."

"Civilized army!" I said. And then I stopped. How could I explain to him how harshly those two words clashed in my mind. I had seen civilization, in my father's town. And I had certainly seen enough of army life. They had nothing to do with each other. In my father's town, men lived in houses, with their own wives, and they fed on food they had grown or bought in the market. They had laws. But why try to teach an old man that his ways are wrong?

So I went on in a different vein. "Don't you see that if he lost the armor, and the contest had gone by rules he had chosen, that would make things even worse? As things are, he can blame

Odysseus for lying to the panel and winning them over with sweet words. Or he can blame Agamemnon for making a private deal with Odysseus. Or he can blame the panel for paying attention to that notorious liar Odysseus. Or he can blame the king's brother for bribing the panel. But if the procedure is really, obviously, fair, and he still loses, that's far worse. Think how much face he loses then!"

I had been walking along behind Nestor, speaking to his back. Now he stopped and turned. "You don't believe in justice?"

"Yes, I do. Back home, in Phrygia, we had justice and the town flourished. Hardly anyone ever had to go into exile over a dispute. We had such good justice, that once the elders had decided a case, everyone accepted it. Even for murder, if the family got its blood gold, we had no more feuding."

"Well, then," Nestor began. But I interrupted him. "This army is not a town. Look how you live, in squalid shelters by the sea, you breed with women you've stolen at spear point. You gorge on food you've plundered. Look how you quarrel among yourselves. You have no homes here. You can leave at a moment's notice, as soon as you get angry. Achilles would not accept anything from Agamemnon. He rejoined the army only because of his love for Patroclus. You're one of them. Why can't you see it? All you soldiers have this crazy thing about honor. You have no sense of fairness or justice. Your honor is a trap. Justice drowns in it."

Nestor was a wise man. He heard me out and quietly said: "I understand you. The younger men here care too much about honor. Some die for it every day and waste their blood. Hector died to save his own honor. Achilles would have let us all die rather than compromise his precious honor. It is a trap, as you say. You are a wise woman, Tecmessa. Tell me what you think we should do. How can we teach Ajax to respect justice above honor?"

"Too late." I said. "He is in a rage over his honor. There is only one thing you can do. Have Agamemnon award him the armor."

"Agamemnon will never agree to that. But Odysseus would, to keep the peace. Why don't I ask him to bring the armor? It is not yet dawn."

"Never. Ajax wants what he deserves, and he wants it from Agamemnon. He has no interest in gifts. In any event, he would never accept anything from Odysseus now. Have you forgotten what you knew about honor? Ajax will never forget. Even after he dies, the memory of his anger will keep some life in him. What is the worst thing one dead ghost can do to another? If his ghost meets the ghost of Odysseus in the underworld, he will do whatever that worst thing is."

He paused. "I will ask Odysseus, nevertheless." I was right, and Nestor knew it, but I thanked him.

I turned and it was dawn. The faint pink along the outline of the mountains had deepened, and the rosy clouds rose in the east like the hand of a great god. When I returned to our shelter, Ajax was gone. I picked up the child, who was still sleeping, and took him to a neighbor's for safety.

Odysseus Explains the Fury of Ajax

That night, Ajax lost his mind. He did it quietly, during the hours he sat waiting for the commanders to bring him back his honor. The rage built in him, like a wave rising in a flume of rock that has no outlet, rising and rising until it explodes in the air. The rage of Ajax was like that.

He had decided to kill Agamemnon and me—Odysseus—and the other commanders. Agamemnon because he had convened the panel of judges and then made the final call on the basis of their decision. Menelaus because he thought Menelaus had bribed the judges. But mostly me, because I had the armor, and because he thought I had tricked the jury with a bunch of clever lies, and because he despised my cleverness.

Ajax was literally out of his mind with anger.

Now here's the part of this story you'll find hardest to believe— unless you've seen how anger builds into madness in a combat soldier. Day after day he sees his friends die. Night after night he sleeps on the edge of fear, especially when the new moon has set on a cloudy night before dawn, and the enemy who might have found their way to his camp by moonlight could now attack in total darkness. Morning after morning again he puts his life on the line. Then suddenly something makes him snap, and he kills anything in his path. Friend or enemy, he does not care. He kills.

That night, they were bringing a flock of captured sheep down to feed the army, and the sheep milled around on the road, blocking Ajax's path. Have you ever tried to walk a narrow way that is blocked by sheep? Ajax lost it. Whatever stood between him and his honor was the enemy in his tormented mind. He started killing sheep. Two big rams he picked out as the commanders. He wounded them, picked up one under each arm, and carried them back to his shelter.

Later, as the sun came up, I followed his tracks from the killing zone back toward his shelter. There I caught sight of him. He was slathered in blood, sheep guts hanging off his shoulders. He had just finished flogging Agamemnon to death—the ram he called Agamemnon—and he had stepped out for a breath of fresh air before setting up to torture Odysseus—me!—that other ram, tied foot to foot by his door, bleating in pain. He was hauling this "Odysseus" into his shelter to string him up on the center pole. He was swearing and cursing. I wept to see it. I was that sorry for him, even though I knew he was cursing me, I knew that he wanted to do those things to me.

It's funny. My gift of words, my cleverness, was part of what gave me the power to understand Ajax and pity him. The very thing he hated me for, that was the thing that allowed me to go on loving him, even now that he was slathered in blood and draped in sheep guts. And he thought those guts were mine.

I could not bear to look. I had nothing to say to him then. He was beyond the reach of my words. Soon, I thought, when the sun is bright enough, he will see what he has done, and then the shame will set in. I went sorrowing back along the shore, looking to tell Agamemnon that he was safe. And Tecmessa, if I could find her, that her husband would need her.

Tecmessa Finds Ajax Has a Gift for Words

I fell in love with my husband for the first time this morning. Before then, I had seen him the way the others did. He was as strong as four ordinary men, so that anywhere in the battle where he was not, they needed a team of four men to replace him. But now I see there is no replacing him. He has a mind, a soul. And he found the words he needed to let us see who he was, after all these years. I suppose he had always seen himself that way—as a big strong ox of a man, so strong he did not need to win any prizes for brains. But this morning he found himself up against an enemy that could not be moved by muscle power, so he found power in his soul.

The enemy was shame and ridicule. His powers were kindness and the mental strength to see things in his own way, despite the laughter of his former friends. He is a better man than anyone knew, and I love him.

After the sun came up this morning, the neighbor women where I was staying offered to take care of my son and urged me to go give comfort to Ajax. They said the whole army was laughing at him—the big lummox who lost his grip and could not tell the difference between a pair of old rams and his enemies.

I found him sitting outside our shelter, staring out to sea. His shield was beside him, and a little farther off a jumble of his armor. His face was no longer a mask. I could read feelings on it—anguish. I had never seen him in mental pain before.

"Bring me my son," he said. At first I was terrified. What would he do with the little boy? Eurysaces was only six years old. Ajax was still caked with dried blood from his rampage among the sheep. "You'll frighten him," I said. "I will give him a gift that will guard him forever," he said. "He is my son; he will not be frightened."

So I sent to my women friends and asked them to bring our son to us. After a few minutes I broke the silence: "What can you do now?" I asked.

He said he was thinking about his home. The laughter of the army would reach Salamis soon enough, and how could he face his father? His father had won every prize there was in the previous war with Troy. So, he said, he could not go home, not unless he did something to bring back his honor in a way that his father would recognize. He could storm the gates of Troy, maybe lose his life there, and gain some honor. But at the cost of doing something good for Agamemnon, whom he then saw as an enemy.

"You must not leave our son," I said. If you die, he and I will be sold as slaves, and the shame you feel today will be nothing to the shame we will feel. Someone will say, "Look at that bedraggled slave woman and her barefoot boy. Can you believe she was once the bedmate of Ajax, the great hero? Can you believe, that boy was the son of a hero and the grandson of a king? Yes, that one, with the shrunken abdomen and the protruding ribs and the scars where he was beaten for begging in the streets." I laid it on thick.

Women are best when they are silent; that is what Ajax believed, and I could see he was thinking of saying that. But he spoke words of comfort instead. "Whatever happens to me, my brother will look after you, and I will see to it that our son has the honor he should have as my son."

Our son's name meant nothing in my language, but it meant "Broadshield" in Greek. He was six years old, large for his size, and he always got along well with his father. He was never afraid of the blood Ajax brought back on his face and hands and weapons—more blood than any of the other fathers.

Broadshield came up behind Ajax then, and without saying a word he hunkered down and lifted a corner of the shield, like a weight lifter, straining from his legs. He got it about a foot off the ground and then dropped it, leaping backward to protect his feet.

Ajax laughed and pulled him onto his lap, folded him in the powerful left arm that held the shield in battle. The shield was as tall as Ajax himself and almost twice as wide. Even Ajax could not run with such a thing on his arm, but then Ajax never ran. Now he laughed again and spoke to the boy.

"You'll be lifting it all the way soon enough. It's yours now. I give it to you."

"How will you fight? You'll have to fight."

"You'll lend it to me, then. I will carry the shield as a loan from my son, and I will think of you as I prop it up and start inching it forward. It terrifies the Trojans."

"It doesn't terrify me."

Ajax laughed a third time, and I knew I loved him then. He squeezed the boy, lifted him, and set him on his feet.

"Good. The man who owns this shield is never terrified."

Then he told me an amazing thing, while the boy practiced lifting corners of the shield. Time passes, he said, time beyond counting, and time brings changes. It brings day after night, spring after winter, calm water after a storm at sea. And to him, he said, time was bringing a change of heart. He had offended the generals; he would make things right with them. He had offended the gods; he would make things right with them, too. It was the most beautiful thing I had ever heard him say.

He would go down to where the river spreads out by the sea, where salt water mixes with fresh, and there in the privacy of the high water plants he would clean his body and his soul, wash his armor, and bury for good the sword with which he had done so much damage earlier that morning.

I have never been happier.

Agamemnon Decides to Strike Fear into the Army

Ajax is a fool. I always thought he was a big dumb ox, but he was dumber than I realized. Why did he have to make such a fuss over that stupid armor? It's half his size. He'll never wear it. Neither will Odysseus. It's too big for him. But Odysseus wants it, and I absolutely have to keep Odysseus happy. It's obvious we can't win the war without his brains. And it's equally obvious that Ajax does not have a brain in his head. He was down for a full 5 percent of the booty from Troy. Nestor estimates a 5 percent share as worth more than ten suits of precious armor. Ajax lost all that when he lost his mind and tried to take my life.

Ajax is also disobedient and disrespectful. All right, yes, he saved my life, but that does not mean he can talk back to me and give me orders. I won't have that kind of behavior. I am glad he lost his mind. Now I can have him killed in good conscience and no one will complain. I will need a bunch of dumb oxes to replace him, but men with shit for brains are as common as fleas on a blanket. He is no great loss. He has friends in the army, I admit. Or he used to. But they can't blame me.

None of this is my fault. I did what I had to do. I followed the custom of the army. Ajax should have accepted that. What a fool!

I have two jobs here. I am commander in chief of the army. That's my first job here at Troy. I have the job because I am king at Mycenae, which is the leading city of Greece. As commander, I give orders. That's tough, because we have other kings here, men like Achilles and Odysseus, who brought their own troops. They had to come because of our alliance, and they had sworn to accept me as commander.

My second job is king. As king, I am *basileus*. That means I am a judge. A judge is charged with maintaining justice among his people. Whenever there is a dispute among them, he renders judgment, and he explains that judgment to the people. If he does his job well, the people on both sides should accept his judgment and go on with their lives, working peacefully together. That is what we kings mean by justice.

Justice comes to us by way of a *basileus*. Its purpose is clear: to allow human beings to stay together in a community through thick and thin. Justice allows us to disagree and then move on. Justice is precious. People like me who give justice should receive the highest honor. And that is why a man who attacks a judge should be punished in the worst possible way. When a man attacks a judge he attacks justice itself, the most precious thing we have.

Ajax attacked me. A man who attacks me will be stoned to death and his body left out for the vultures and wild dogs. That's been the law for generations. And it is entirely fair: a crime worse than murder calls for a penalty worse than death. That enormous gross body of Ajax's—all those overgrown muscles—that body is going to lie out and rot where the whole army can smell it, whatever parts the jackals don't eat. They can smell him and learn again the old lesson. Never attack the king. If you do you will die in disgrace and your body will be disgraced. You will be a piece of stinking rubbish.

They all need to learn to be afraid of the king. If I do nothing else I will teach the army to fear me.

Nestor Proposes a Detour, to the Same Destination

I say this with great sadness, but I have to admit that you are right, Agamemnon. Well, right as to what has to be done in this case. The traditional penalty for trying to assassinate the high king is death by stoning, after which the body is left out to be the plaything of wild dogs and vultures. Death alone is not harsh enough for a dangerous rebel. Justice demands no less than this of the king: a king must act swiftly and surely to avert further attacks on his body. That is because the king is the embodiment of justice, and justice is what keeps society from flying apart into dangerous fragments. Fragments of society are dangerous to each other, because they fight each other. But they are even more dangerous to themselves, because they are too small to survive the dangers of this world.

Justice is at stake, the very existence of justice hangs in the balance. Think what this means. Justice is more important than food or water or shelter or sex or anything else that people want. Without justice, friendships break up like boats on sharp rocks. Without justice, quarreling would burst through our army like wildfire. Without justice, honor is meaningless. You may enjoy your honor only so long as you have a community that honors you. But without justice, the community is lost, and there will be no one left to give you honor. Without justice, you cannot be sure of having any good thing for more than a day. Your family, your livelihood, even your life is at risk, if justice goes away.

Justice requires good judges, along with a people who treat their judges with respect. Some people will never learn the value of justice. Some people are so fixed in their little minds on one good thing or another that they are deaf and blind to justice. And those people should be driven out of the community to live alone like beasts. Or, better, they should be killed. Because we human beings do not do well as separate individuals. We are not the kind of beast that can range the mountains in solitary strength. We always find groups to join. But if we are unable to respect justice, we have no place in a group. And without a place in a group, a human being has no place anywhere.

Nevertheless, I am concerned about the effect of this penalty on the army. They all cherish Ajax, and stoning him will be hard for them. Before we go any further, we need to ensure that they accept the justice of the penalty. Otherwise, they might turn away from you, and the penalty might actually weaken you, rather than strengthen your rule.

So I came here to offer you advice as soon as I heard how Ajax had set out to kill you. Look at you! You are pacing around so nervously. Why is that? Do you suppose I think this is your fault? I really don't. But I think you could have prevented it.

No, no, not by giving Ajax the armor. Everyone in the army knows he does not deserve it. Even the women and boys. You are right. You can't do a thing like that. Who would ever trust you again? But if your procedure had been just, and if it had given the armor to Ajax…

Yes, yes, of course, some people would complain that the procedure was flawed. Perhaps everybody, since everybody seems to think the prize should go to Odysseus. But I did not come here to be playing games of "if only" with you. The past cannot be recalled. The question is what to do now. I am told that you have sent troops to arrest him. I hear also that he has gone to the shore to make his peace with the gods. And, as he promises, to make peace with you.

Now here is the hard question: When he is captured, what do you plan to do? What did you intend when you sent out your men to arrest him? His death of course, in the end. A public stoning. A public shaming of his body afterward? I agree, that is precisely what justice and tradition require. The hard question is how to go about this so that the army agrees with us.

I quite agree, sir. Of course you are right. If you blink, and look away, and people see that you are afraid to exact the full penalty, won't they believe that you have become weak? So weak that rebellion might win? Rebellion is the death of justice. Therefore the end for rebellion must be death. And worse. I agree to all that.

"What's worse than death?" you ask. Shame is worse. Undying shame. That is what strikes fear into the hearts of rebels. Surely I do see how shame protects society. And fear. Though fear is a two-edged weapon. It can turn men into rebels. It can make the men see you as a tyrant. Think differently! Don't fly into a rage and make a rash decision.

Agamemnon Calls for a Trial

I am no tyrant. I care about justice. But you keep saying things like this—as if going about this the wrong way would make me a tyrant.

As if anyone really believed that justice had more to do with *how* we decided than with *what* we decided to do. I don't agree with you at all. But, you are right this far. Ajax has been hugely popular, and I have to think about what they will say afterward in the army.

Are you saying that I should not make the decision on my own, even if it is just?

Yes, yes, I thought you were. That's my Nestor. Procedure above all. You have told me many times what you think: no decision is just if it is made the way a tyrant decides. You want me to decide about how this decision is to be made and by whom.

All right. If it makes you happy I will summon a panel of soldiers to judge the issue. Almost certainly they will vote to exact the full penalty.

Yes, yes. I thought that is what you wanted. And now I see it gives me a huge advantage: they all love Ajax so much, if—all by myself—I decide to have him stoned and shamed, I will get the blame.

So let the army decide. That gets me off the hook. That's what you mean by acting like a king, not a tyrant? The tyrant makes tough decisions, the king gets other people to do the dirty work for him? You are a wise man, Nestor. Let others decide.

Tecmessa Finds the Body

We should not have left Ajax alone. I realized that soon after he left, as soon as I had time to think back over what he had said. I do not blame myself; he was so persuasive. I do not blame him; what he told me was true, every word, but he made it so easy for me to misunderstand. He was in that calm state that people who are tormented find when they decide to make peace with the world through self-sacrifice. He was relieved, almost happy. I caught his tone and I sang with it.

I should have remembered how calm and happy my uncle was, the day before he conquered his wasting disease with his own hand. He had just the strength left to do it, and once he decided he was at peace. After that we no longer worried about him; and when we were not watching him, he took his life.

Ajax would never take his life if his wife or his soldiers were with him. So we fanned out along the shore, the soldiers scouring the beaches north and south. I wanted to be the first to find him, so I ran to the one spot I knew he would choose, where the open land near the sea is broken by high grass and sedge along the Scamander where it spreads toward the salt water, and the tall water plants would shield him from our eyes. I knew he would want so much privacy for his death.

And I knew we had a little time. Ajax never did anything fast. He was never a runner. When I parted the sedge and found him he was still warm.

I had wailed for my father and mother and for my brothers, years ago. I had beaten my breast and torn my hair as I knew I should and as I felt like doing at the time. But now, over Ajax, I had no wailing left in me.

I knew we had to conceal the death as long as possible. We were all vulnerable, once the commanders knew that he was gone. Ajax himself was most vulnerable, dead and unburied. They would hate his dead body as much as they had hated the living man. They would abuse it and shame it, too, if they could. And there was no one to protect him except me and his soldiers, and they would be demoralized. No one but us, till his brother Teucer could come down from the hills, and Teucer was only a bow-and-arrow man. The Greeks hardly counted Teucer as a man anyway, because he had been a bastard son, and because he did not stand and fight with a spear.

So I sat beside Ajax's warm body until his soldiers came and set up a shout. That brought Agamemnon's soldiers, led by his brother Menelaus. But Ajax's soldiers made a barricade around his body, and there was a standoff. Soon after, by good luck, Ajax's brother Teucer came down from his hunt in the hills, with a few men, and he took command of the soldiers of Ajax. At the same time, Agamemnon himself heaved on the scene. Of the three great enemies of Ajax, only Odysseus was missing to make the horror complete.

Then I saw a small figure that Teucer had brought with him. My son.

Odysseus Saves Ajax's Honor

Ajax was the army. He stood for all the men who put their lives on the line every day out of loyalty and friendship and because they cared about their honor and did not ever wish to be shamed. He was bigger in body than any of us, and more loyal, and he cared more for his honor. Some say he cared too much for his honor. But I do not agree. Caring about his honor was what made him such a magnificent soldier and such a loyal friend. When the commanders shamed him, he wanted to kill them. And when the gods shamed him again by driving him out of his mind, when the gods made a public display of this great soldier reduced to attacking woolly sheep, of course he wanted to kill himself. Some say he went too far, that he cared too much about shame. But I do not think so. Taking his death into his own hands—that was the only way he could reclaim his honor in the sight of all.

What can a soldier do when the officers bring shame on him? Maybe he could go home. Achilles wanted to go home, and he would have done that, too, if Hector had not killed the man he loved, Patroclus. But Ajax could not go home. His father would have disowned him.

So, short of going home, what could a soldier do? What I see all the time—he can do very, very little. He does the very least he can get away with. Takes the smallest risks. Withdraws into his own shell, or into a band of friends who help each other stay out of battle—and out of trouble. So the soldiers keep their minds free and obey their orders in the smallest possible way—just enough so they are not punished, but not enough to do any good in the war. And they do exactly what they are told—not a bit more—while holding in their hearts hatred for their commanders. But Ajax could not do that. He was too honest a man.

So Ajax withdrew in the only way that was left to him, and I honor him for it. He did what I might. No, I would not have done that. I want to go home. I have a home to go to, as he did not. I would give every last shred of honor, if necessary, so that I could go home to the island and be with my wife. Maybe, if you are as clever as I am, you can do without honor. There will be no honor in the way I plan to win the war for the Greeks. But you can't run an army on my example. Somehow, you must retain the loyalty and the enthusiasm of the regular troops. And they care about honor.

If you can't work out a way to hold onto Ajax, you can't hold onto your army at all. That is what Agamemnon never understood. In his shelter, the night before we lost Ajax, I remember Agamemnon said this: "A great ox can be controlled with a very small goad." That meant he thought he could control Ajax the way a farmer controls an ox.

Agamemnon is a fool. No commander controls any of his troops the way a farmer drives a team of oxen. Oxen don't need spirit. Soldiers do. Even if the soldiers march where you tell them to march and wave their spears at your command, you may not be in control. They may have drawn back into their own minds or into their small circles of friends, and then you have lost the most important part of them. Ajax is not an ox. No soldier is an ox. A commander needs to be the leader of the whole soldier, mind, body, and spirit. This is called "paying attention to morale."

Agamemnon thinks that so long as he does what he believes is right, or follows the rules handed down by tradition, he is acting like a king, and the troops will follow him. Nestor thinks if kings follow procedures, and if they do not put themselves too blatantly above the law, that's enough justice for an army or a city. They are both fools. We are human, we are not rational, we are passionate about honor and shame. Real justice, human justice, must pay attention to this. Justice should not try to be any more rational than we are.

****

When the army began to stream down to the shore to watch the face-off between Agamemnon and Ajax's brother Teucer, I followed them. I saw the body, with the little boy and his mother kneeling over it, as if their presence would deter the ferocity of the king. Teucer's and Ajax's troops were lined up between the body and the beach, where Menelaus had drawn up his unit. Menelaus and Teucer were shouting insults at each other. I thought Agamemnon was about to give the order to seize the body; Teucer had notched an arrow to his string.

Agamemnon was prepared to use violence to prevent the family from burying Ajax. He was in the right, so far as our traditions of justice go. He was following an old rule. The rule is: shame his body because he was a rebel. But there is another rule: honor his body because he saved your life. And another: honor his body because he was a rebel who had been loyal to you until you treated him with contempt. Or my favorite rule of all: honor his body because he was Ajax. A onetime rule.

But there was no time to argue about rules. The fighting was about to begin, and everyone would lose by it. Teucer and most of his men would die. The woman and the boy would be sold off as slaves. Ajax's body would rot in a ravine, whatever shreds of it had not fed the crows. Agamemnon and the rest of us would be left to fight at Troy—if we still cared to follow him. But the army's love for Ajax would surge back, and after that would come renewed disgust over Agamemnon's rule. I would go home. So would others. Troy would stand. There would be no booty for any of us.

So I stood in front of Agamemnon and gave the shortest speech of my life:

"You know that he was the best of us in the field, every day. He was honor-driven to give of himself whatever you asked. He saved your life when the ships were burning. He saved mine, more than once. And for this you gave him no reward, but you called him, behind his back, a dumb ox. So he was honor-driven—by you, lord of men. You drove him to rebel.

"Now he and his family are helpless. That body could be yours or mine, if the gods went after us the way they went after Ajax. Now he depends on us to save him. There is no greater dishonor than to be refused burial. From that, there is no recovery. It could be you. You yourself could be damned by an unkind king to an eternity of shame. Let his family bury him, and perhaps the gods will be kinder to you than they were to him."

Agamemnon said, "So this is just about me? I thought I was supposed to take thought for the whole army. But you tell me to think about myself. You say this could be me."

"Yes, if you want to think of it that way," I answered.

He turned and ordered his troops back to the camp. Menelaus went with them. The family stayed to attend to the corpse and prepare for the burial. Tecmessa stood and bowed her head to me. Teucer thanked me and asked me quietly to leave. I understood. Though I held myself blameless toward Ajax, the family saw me as an agent of the trouble that had come upon them. And so I left the body of my former friend without further ceremony. The family and his soldiers remained on the beach, alone.

PART THREE

Learning from the Ajax Story

A New Approach to Justice and Compassion

The garlands wither on your brow;
       Then boast no more your mighty deeds.
Upon Death's purple altar now,
       See where the victor-victim bleeds.
           Your heads must come
           To the cold tomb.
Only the actions of the just
Smell sweet, and blossom in their dust.

    —From JAMES SHIRLEY's "DIRGE," the conclusion to *The Contention of Ajax and Ulysses* (c. 1640, pub. 1659)

The story packs two surprises. The big lunk Ajax has a mind, and he knows how to use words well. As for the cunning Odysseus, he has a heart; he is capable of deep compassion.

Compassion may help when justice fails. Perhaps we should forget justice and show compassion to Ajax instead—just enough compassion to keep him happily at work on our behalf. That might be the strategy of the elementary school track and field day, which allows there to be many winners and no losers; everyone is awarded a prize. But then prizes and rewards lose their meaning. A consolation prize is an insult to an adult.

Justice and compassion appear to be at war with each other. To give people what they deserve, as justice seems to require, you must set compassion aside. To prevent suffering, as compassion seems to require, you must set justice aside. Justice, as most people understand it, is not supposed to take people's feelings into account. It is supposed simply to do what is right.

That cannot be correct. Justice is supposed to settle disputes, to bring us together in a peaceful community. You can't bring us together by ignoring our feelings. Besides, we admire compassion, and we should all know that someday each one of us will depend on the compassion of others. If compassion is good, and justice really forbids compassion, then—in those cases—justice would be bad and wrong. But justice is supposed to be good.

How to cut through this tangle? I will distinguish between two closely related concepts, which I will call "justice" and "fairness." Fairness does indeed forbid compassion, while justice does not. On the theory I propose, justice sometimes calls us to set fairness aside in the name of compassion.

I want to understand justice in such a way that it is fully compatible with compassion. If justice is going to help us get along, it has to affect our feelings. And if justice is a quality of character, it must be about feelings, because that's where character is—in the feelings that help us do well or poorly. In the last analysis, I will argue, justice and compassion come down to the same thing—to a sort of human wisdom. That is the thesis of this little book.

Fairness and justice are truly at war with one another. Fairness is not wise. Fairness is following principles wherever they may lead, regardless of people's feelings. Fairness is a trap in which justice and compassion die, where members of a team are hurt beyond repair. Yet fairness has often been thought to be the heart of justice. That cannot be correct. The heart of justice is wisdom.

Wisdom is a quality of leaders. It is not so mysterious as you may think, but it cannot be delivered by a formula. Being wise, a leader pays attention to others and sets an example for the leaders who report to him. The sort of action that is wise in one situation may be foolish in another. A wise leader may have a reason in mind that calls for action today and inaction tomorrow.

A dilemma is a problem that cannot be resolved. All the choices open to the king at this point are wrong. That does not mean the king is off the hook. His failure to be a leader is to blame for getting the army into this mess. Had he been a better king, he would have had better choices available, and the human factors with which he must work would have been in better shape for him to work through the dilemma.

I offer no rule for solving this dilemma, because I believe there is none. If there were a rule for handling Ajax and Odysseus, then the army would not need leadership; it would not need to have discussions; it would not need anyone to make decisions. All it would need would be a boss who understands the rule and applies it, like a student working out binomial expansions by a method she has memorized. Algorithms require no leadership. Justice does. There can be no justice in a community without the good atmosphere that leadership can create.

Justice is a kind of human wisdom that is shared by members of a community. When justice is present, the community has the capacity to settle disputes in such a way that anger goes away, or at least that anger falls back far enough that the members of the community can work together. That succeeds only when the individuals involved have justice in their souls—what I call "psychological justice." In a soul where the wisdom of justice is present, compassion and respect are there too; they are a moderating influence on the springs of anger, on the love of honor, and on the fear of shame. In such a well-tempered soul, desire and anger are born with limited power. There is nothing in a well-tempered soul that would incline a person to destroy the community for the sake of personal advantage.

Put this way, my thesis is frightfully abstract. No one has a soul that is so well tempered all the time. And many of us hardly ever have our desires and ambitions in balance. Some will do anything for power, others will do anything for profit. And we know that no arrangements we make in society protect us from predatory fellow citizens, from mutual hatred, from tensions that simmer in the direction of civil war. The justice we have does not work as we want it to. The justice I wrote about in the preceding paragraph is an ideal—something we can think about but cannot expect to have on this earth.

But this book is not abstract. It's not about how to design a constitution, or how to make laws. The ideas of this book apply to where we live—at the level of a team, a workplace, or a department. This is the justice of our everyday lives: Who gets a promotion or a raise? Who gets the corner office? Who gets the largest bonus at the end of the year? And also which child inherits the violin, or the antique lace, or the money?

This book is about what we can do to make our justice work a little better—not perfectly, just better. In the end, this is a book about leadership, because that's what we need if we are to survive with the imperfect justice we can have. By "leadership" I do not mean management or any other use of rank or authority. I have often seen the lowest-ranking member of a team show leadership by setting an example, sometimes shaming higher-ranking people into doing what is best for all.

Leadership is easiest to spot when it's not there. Leadership is what Agamemnon does not have. He has authority: people obey him. And he has knowledge: he knows what tradition requires, and he thinks he knows what is right. But rank and knowledge do not make a leader. Agamemnon is lucky in having a wise adviser, the old man Nestor. Nestor wants the king to follow procedures, and, yes, that would make Agamemnon a better king. But he could be a much better king and still not be a leader in my sense. Following procedures by itself will not make Agamemnon a leader.

| The Myth

The ancient Greeks used their myths. Myths were not treasures to be kept sacred. Anyone could put fingerprints on a myth, tell it in his or her own way. Poets used myth as a rich vein to mine for narratives; wise people generally used myth for stories that they could mold to serve as illustrations for points they wanted to make. That is what I am doing in these pages, retelling the story of Ajax to make a point about justice and its relation to compassion. Because the point is about the way a community depends on these two virtues, I have wanted to present the story from different points of view. This is a modern technique, but it owes much to the ancient tradition of inventing speeches in twos or fours to bring out various perspectives on an issue.[1]

The story I tell in these pages derives from Sophocles' play *Ajax,* for which I have followed Meineck's fine translation. Sophocles leaves much unsaid and unexplained, as in all his plays, and, most important, unjudged. He leaves to his audience the pleasure of judging such questions as whether or not Ajax's claim was treated fairly by the army, and whether or not Ajax lied to his wife about his intention to take his life. I have taken positions on some of these, not by way of interpreting the play but in order to illustrate the moral and political issues this story can bring to life.

The play begins after Ajax's attempt to kill the commanders has been foiled by madness, so that the action of the play begins when Ajax comes to his senses and realizes what he has done. I have imagined a number of scenes that are set before the start of the play. My work is not an interpretation of the play; it is a new work, using some of the play's material, aiming at a clarity that the play does not give us. Sophocles delivers no ethical verdicts, nor does he pursue issues of ethical theory. He raises questions that provoke me to do both of those.

Strength, loyalty, and friendship—these are the words to keep in mind for Ajax. He is the muscles of the army. He is a man of few words, but he is not slow or dull. He has always been where he was needed, protecting his friends behind the wall of his great bulk and his enormous shield. Among the lives he has saved is that of Odysseus—the brains of the army. "Send for Odysseus," they would say, when an eloquent speech was required. And "send for Odysseus," they would whisper, when they needed a devious plan, a trick, or a spy in the citadel of the enemy. But whenever the battle was joined, and Greek soldiers were in danger, no one needed to call Ajax. He was there, to help his friends, and he was huge, strong, comforting.

When Achilles flew into a rage and resolved to leave the war, the commanders sent Odysseus to speak for them, to persuade Achilles to give up his anger in return for rewards promised by Agamemnon. Achilles saw the cleverness behind Odysseus's speech, and so he did not believe a word of it. He suspected that Agamemnon's promise was false, and, in any case, Odysseus's cleverness was itself a reason for suspicion. Achilles probably felt that a speaker with a sound cause would have no need of cleverness. Others spoke, after Odysseus, but it was the one who came last who made the difference—Ajax.

Ajax had never needed to be clever. His cause was sound and simple. With a few hard words, he reminded Achilles of their friendship, and that was enough. Because of Ajax, Achilles would stay, though he made no promise to fight.

And now Achilles is dead. His armor, the gift of the god who made it, is now a prize for the most valuable soldier in the army, the ancient equivalent of the MVP. Sophocles is vague about how Agamemnon decided the issue, but he gives several clues that he turned the matter over to something like a jury of the peers of Ajax and Odysseus—a procedure familiar to Sophocles' audience, which would have expected fine speeches to be delivered on both sides before a large panel of jurors chosen by lot.

However the decision is reached, it is decided that the armor will go to Odysseus. Brains beat brawn, as so often happens. Ajax cannot accept the decision. He flies into a rage, worse than Achilles'; he becomes insane with anger. He tries to kill the commanders, but in his madness he takes after a flock of sheep instead, torturing and killing the helpless beasts.

Sophocles begins the plot of his play at this point, after Ajax's anger has already swept him across a line from which there can be no return. A soldier who has attempted to kill his commanders cannot live. A soldier who has been thrice shamed has no reason to live. Ajax was shamed when he lost the prize, shamed when he failed to kill the commanders, and shamed again when he was found out, running amok among the sheep.

Sophocles' story is about the death and burial of Ajax, but I wanted to begin mine much earlier. I wanted to imagine how they break the news to Ajax that the decision has gone against him, and how they try to keep him on the team afterward. This is the unwritten scene, which I develop in the opening pages of part II.

As I tell the story, Odysseus understands the loss of Ajax as a disaster for the army, but more, as a blow to him personally. The idea that Odysseus felt compassion for Ajax comes as a surprise at the beginning of Sophocles' version of the story; Athena, to whom Odysseus expresses his feelings, is surprised, and so would we be if we were in the ancient audience. Compassion (as felt by the ancient Greeks) was a pain felt personally on behalf of someone similar enough to oneself that one could easily imagine the same suffering falling upon oneself.[2]

The idea that Odysseus loved Ajax, however, is my contribution, but one that the old stories make plausible. Ajax was a lovable character.

Notes

1. The Ajax-Odysseus debate was a popular subject among ancient writers. A composition by Antisthenes has survived and is translated in Gagarin and Woodruff (1995), pp. 167–172. Antisthenes (c. 455–360) was a student of Socrates who wrote in Athens in the early fourth century BCE. A more elaborate debate, with an account of Ajax's suicide, is found in Ovid's *Metamorphoses*, 13.1–480. Here are some choice lines from each side of Ovid's debate:

Ajax:
But why give them to the Ithacan, who operates
Unarmed, by stealth, and by tricking the enemy?

The glint of gold on Achilles' helmet would only
Give away his hiding place, not that his head
Could ever bear the weight.

Odysseus:
Your total worth is all in your bulk, mine in my mind.
And as much as the pilot surpasses the rower,
So much greater am I than you. In our lives
The head counts for more than the hand,
And in our intelligence our existence lies.

                    —Lombardo, 13.120–124 and 442–447

The poet James Shirley wrote a verse drama based on Ovid's story in the mid-1600s. Of this, the most famous part is the concluding "Dirge" (quoted on p. 61 above).

2. *Ajax* 121–126. On the scene see Knox (1979); on the gods' lack of compassion, see Konstan (2001).

Caring about Ajax

Odysseus speaks first in my narrative. He has won the contest but lost a friend, and he knows that this is not the way a contest should end.

The story he has to tell here is sad in many ways, sad for Ajax and for all who loved him. But it is also sad about justice and compassion and friendship. All the good things failed for Ajax and Odysseus. Good things are not supposed to fail, so we need to ask what went wrong.

But something is going right in the story. It reveals itself in Odysseus's attitude toward Ajax. This is a stunning surprise in the play by Sophocles: Odysseus, the famous trickster, the man who will do anything to win, the man who invented the Trojan Horse—this man cares about Ajax.

Ajax used to be lovable enough, but now he has changed. The lovable, loyal, hardworking soldier has transformed himself into a furious killing machine, driven by the anger that grew from shame and dishonor. He was always a man who cared about honor, who did the honorable thing again and again, and was honored for what he did. But now Odysseus's victory in the contest has put him to shame. The more you care about honor, the worse it hurts to be put to shame. And shame leads to anger—anger at those who shamed you, anger at those who saw you being shamed, and anger at yourself for being shamed. Ajax's love of honor was prodigious, and so, therefore, was his anger.

"Silly old Greek!" you want to say. "We are so much better off than he was; we, at least, do not have to live in a primitive culture that makes so much of honor and shame."

Think again. He was no sillier than we are. Many of the disputes we experience daily over rewards and compensation are all about shame and honor. In a philosophy department, Professor X is angry to find that a colleague who has published less than he is making a higher salary; or Professor Y is angry that Professor X is well paid while giving no attention to teaching. "No one respects the time and energy I put into my students," Professor Y fumes. Perhaps his honor will be satisfied if he is given a major teaching award. Little of this has been about the buying power of a salary; it has mostly been about shame and honor.

Consider the difference in a university between the staff who provide student services and the faculty who bring glory through research. In hard times, staff jobs will be cut and salaries frozen or diminished through furloughs, while the most distinguished faculty will be untouched or rewarded. Top faculty are irreplaceable and essential to what the university perceives as its mission; student services staff can be replaced or eliminated with no damage to the rankings of the various departments. Budget cuts of this kind show these loyal hard workers that they are outliers in the university community. They are hurt when they are deprived of money, but they are hurt more grievously by the realization that they do not count for much. They are Ajax.

Take the case of the banker and the autoworker. The worker really does not have enough buying power; but what angers her most about the whopping bonus the banker received is that it insults the hard work she has done; she has a sense of injustice, and she needs money, but her sense of injustice is tuned more closely to her to her need for respect than it is to her need for money. "I work hard every day and barely break even; he just had a few clever ideas and makes off with a fortune. They—the bosses—insult me. They say I can quit and be replaced; they say they don't ever want the banker to quit; that is why they need to give him all that money. It's worse than unfair." She too is Ajax.

She is right. This is worse than unfair because of the damage to her personal sense of honor. It is devastating to be told that you are disposable, while other people are not. We are no better than the old Greeks on this: we care about honor too, and we should.

In the previous paragraphs, I have been trying to overcome a barrier to feeling compassion for Ajax—the barrier that rises between us and people whom we think are very different from us because they have feelings that make no sense to us. The ancient Greeks believed that compassion arises from a felt recognition of common vulnerability. When Odysseus pities Ajax, he does so because, as he says in Sophocles' play (Meineck's translation):

> I pity the poor man
> Yoked to this insatiable evil,
> Even though he is my enemy.
> It could just as easily have been me.
> We are all insubstantial shadows,
> And life is just a flickering dream. (lines 121–126)

Odysseus knows that he too could lose his mind in anger, and we know he will, when he has been shamed by the presence of the suitors in his palace and the hospitality of his maidservants. He will slay them all without pity, men and women, and sling up the maidservants like clothes on a line—an action for which the townspeople will want to hold him accountable. Perhaps traumatized old soldiers are especially prone to such murderous anger, but we are all vulnerable. It could have been me, or you.

Along with this compassion, Odysseus brings respect for Ajax's honor. That will show to special advantage when the time comes to bury Ajax with full honors.

Odysseus is like the quarterback who has respect for the offensive line. He accepts his fame with its huge rewards; on the other hand he is acutely aware of his own vulnerability. He knows in his gut why he needs the screen of men in front of him. So Odysseus: he knows why he needs Ajax, and he understands why he must treat Ajax with respect, even though he knows that an Ajax is easier to replace than an Odysseus.[1]

Note

1. Contrast Odysseus against the anti-Ajaxes we also frequently encounter—people who demand more honor than is their due (the professor who leaves in a huff because he has been outvoted, enraged because his vote counts no more than anyone else's, even though he has published more books). Ajax is not one of these; he really is the best fighter, as Odysseus is the best strategist. On Ajax's prowess, see Athena's remark at *Ajax* 119–120 and Odysseus's judgment: "I have to admit he was the best fighter of all of us" (line 1340, Meineck).

| The Storytellers

Odysseus

Odysseus in this version of the story, derived from Sophocles, is a man of deep reverence and compassion. This is Homer's Odysseus—a soldier who cares about community, who keeps the army together when it was about to spin into disorder (*Iliad* 2), and who cares more about restoring his home than about sex with a beautiful goddess (*Odyssey* 1). He is not the selfish trickster that Ajax takes him to be, although Sophocles' audience would have known this less attractive Odysseus from stories that came to be told after Homer.

He is a trickster, for all that—just not a selfish one. His stratagems on behalf of the army are, after all, what win him the prize. And he is also a brilliant speaker who knows how to say the right thing at the right moment to save the day—even for a malefactor—in a court of law. In this case, there is no time for a trial; he must speak to prevent a battle on the beach, and he does so, choosing exactly the right words for the moment, what the Greeks of Sophocles' time called *kairos*.

He has no principles, and he abides by no rules. The old stories all show Odysseus as a man who will do whatever it takes to achieve his ends, in view of the circumstances at hand. This Odysseus, although unprincipled, is not a bad man. As he comes to us from Homer's *Iliad* through Sophocles, Odysseus is quite a good man, because the ends he pursues are unselfish. He is not out for number one but for the larger community. Because he acts well consistently without doing so from principle, Odysseus is what I will call a "*particularist*."[1]

To Sophocles' audience, Odysseus probably stood for sophists like Protagoras, who invented the concept of *kairos*, knew how to strengthen an argument on either side of a case, and was a pragmatist on moral and political questions (though probably not a downright relativist).[2]

Compassion comes easily to Odysseus *because* he has no principles. Principles are an obstacle to compassion. This is one of the main themes of this little book. It is illustrated here in the behavior of Odysseus, and it is defended in the argument of part IV: if you wish to nourish compassion in your heart, do not cling to principles.

Justice is supposed to be the virtue that maintains peace, but justice has been a frequent cause for war, probably because the word "justice" for many people stands for principles that must be defended at all costs. The poet William Stafford wrote of "the sickness of lusting after justice."[3] This is a sickness that does not infect Odysseus.

Agamemnon

Agamemnon speaks for justice as he understands it from his position as king and commander in chief. Stories about the Trojan War present him as having features later associated with tyrants: he is selfish, afraid of rebellion from the ranks, and a famously poor loser.[4] He is, nevertheless, a legitimate king who takes kingship very seriously. But as a king at war, he is uprooted from the social context in which he would be more hedged in by law and tradition. Kings in ancient Greece were traditionally commanders at war; often their peacetime powers at home were diminished.

The *Iliad* and all the stories derived from it show a profound difference between people at war and people at peace: on the one hand, we hear about the settled virtues of the polis, the city-state of Troy, with its organized family structures; on the other, we have the Greek army camped out on the beach by its ships, living without families in crude shelters, sleeping with captured women, brawling over the booty taken in war. It is a fine and uniquely Greek irony that the founding poem of Greek culture shows the Greeks less civilized than the barbarian Trojans.

Agamemnon commands an international force. He is king in Mycenae, Odysseus has been ruler in Ithaca, and Ajax comes from the royal house in Salamis. Agamemnon holds our two antagonists as allies and subordinates at the same time, and this ambiguity complicates his attempts to do justice. But don't think the international character of his command undermines the usefulness of his example. Community is especially important when it is wider than the boundaries of a kingdom. And wherever we need community, we need justice, which is its foundation. Justice is precious.

Agamemnon rightly holds that his followers will lose trust in him as commander if he makes decisions that are plainly unjust. As I imagine him, this makes him immune to compassion. Sophocles paints him in colors similar to those of Creon in *Antigone*, who rightly observes that justice (understood in terms of principles) requires him to treat family members like any other citizens. In a just society, there is one law for everyone. Creon will not abridge the law for his niece; Agamemnon will not abridge it for his loyal associate Ajax—even though Ajax has saved his life.

This line of thought leads Agamemnon to a view of justice as defined by outcomes that are determined, on the basis of rules, to be just. It is the duty of the king not only to secure just outcomes on the basis of rules but to persuade the parties on both sides of any dispute to accept the result.[5]

Agamemnon's rule for rewards is that the biggest reward goes to the most valuable soldier; his rule for determining who this is requires him to use a judicial model. For these reasons, he believes that if Ajax respected justice, he would accept the verdict and go back to soldiering.

In the second case that arises in the story, the rule is that the penalty for rebellion against the king is death without the honor of a burial. If justice is a matter of principle, and if Odysseus were a just individual, he would accept that outcome on the basis of the traditional rule, even for his old friend Ajax. So Agamemnon believes.

Both Ajax and Odysseus, however, will refuse to accept Agamemnon's justice, and they have reasons for their refusal, reasons that Agamemnon ought to respect. On Agamemnon's own view, if he were a good king, he would be able to reach an outcome for which he could also win the acceptance of both sides, by persuasion. The Agamemnon of Homer is notoriously poor as a persuader; that is why he depends heavily on Odysseus. Sophocles follows Homer in this, and I have followed Sophocles. Even if

Agamemnon had been right on all counts, he would not have been a strong enough king to win a case before the people.

Nestor

Nestor is the proverbial wise old man of the story. He imagines that he understands justice in terms of procedures governed by principles of fairness. I shall call his the "fairness view." Agamemnon was mainly concerned with finding the right answer and then persuading people to accept it. Nestor is more concerned with the way answers are reached—with basic principles of justice in decision making. He offers a simple rule: if both sides accept the procedure, then justice requires them to accept the result. This is an elementary social contract theory, belonging to the family of theories that gave birth to most modern thinking about political justice or fairness.

The Nestor of my version is, I confess, an anachronism. In ancient Greek thought, the social contract was part of an argument against taking justice seriously: if all we have to go on for justice is an agreement we made, then justice has no solid basis in what is right, and, in that case, we do no real wrong if we violate justice and get away with it. The underlying idea here is that the contract story shows justice to be merely a matter of convention (*nomos*), whereas a moral term that really had a grip on us would be based in nature (*phusis*).[6]

I have chosen to imagine Nestor as holding the fairness view simply so I could get that into the mix. Like Agamemnon's view, Nestor's view does not hold up well in the Ajax example. There are two reasons for this.

The first is that views about fairness have to be neutral on questions of value (so that persons with different values can agree on the fairness of procedures that govern decisions).[7] But the issue in the Ajax case is precisely one of value. You cannot choose a fair way to decide who is the most valuable player unless you agree on what "valuable" means. As we shall see, different procedures bias the case toward different values. But value is what is at issue here. And neither Nestor nor anyone else has proposed a principle of fairness that would answer the question, What is value?

The second reason for the failure of Nestor's approach goes to the heart of the issue of rewards. Rewards are honors (whatever other values they may have), and the proper allocation of honors is a matter of respect. For respect to fill its social purpose it must be felt as respect. But fairness alone does not guarantee respect.

Tecmessa

Tecmessa does not have the privilege of marriage to Ajax; she is a spear-bride, captured from a city in Asia Minor and claimed by Ajax as part of his share of the booty. She is, therefore, in an especially vulnerable position. With Ajax out of the picture, she could be claimed by another soldier and treated as a slave.

Tecmessa illustrates the human cost of the passion for justice as Agamemnon understands it, but she is never a passive victim. As Sophocles presents her, she is a woman of uncommon intelligence, bravery, and resource. She speaks of ineluctable fate, but she uses every means at her disposal to try to save Ajax. Bucking against her destiny, she urges Ajax to accept his fate calmly.

Sophocles does not underscore the irony in this, but he makes it evident enough. He has made Tecmessa one of his most interesting women characters.

I have imagined Tecmessa as taking a position different from that of any of the men with respect to honor, compassion, and justice. The men (with the exception of Odysseus) take honor as a value, without question, and approve of any flight from shame. Tecmessa despises a soldier's honor, along with the anger and fear that rise up in the soldiers who (she believes) care too deeply about guarding their honor.

Odysseus shows compassion in Sophocles' play, but Tecmessa (as I have imagined her) understands two crucial facts about compassion—two reasons why appeals to compassion fail. First, Agamemnon, as a ruler charged with dispensing justice, will believe that he ought not to be moved by pleas of compassion, and so she wisely builds her plea on different ground. Second, she appreciates the feelings of those who expect to receive justice and would resent compassion. Ajax wants what he believes he deserves, not as a result of compassion but as what is rightfully his.

I have invented the scene in Agamemnon's shelter; Tecmessa would have been out of line to speak up at a meeting of men, as would any woman in ancient Greece, especially a woman of her low status. But the circumstances imagined here are unusual, and the men may well have wanted to use Tecmessa's charms to soothe Ajax.

Tecmessa stands for survival above all, especially the survival of the family. She is, in this, the female counterpart of Odysseus. She will argue for whatever will give her family a chance of going forward. The advice she gives Agamemnon, however, is aimed at the survival of the larger community—at helping the commander keep the whole army together.

Notes

1. For particularism, see Dancy (2004). A particularist is a holist with regard to reasons: whether a given consideration is a reason for action or approval depends on a structure of reasons. The same kind of consideration could, in different circumstances, count for or against the same kind of action. For our case, Odysseus's example is this: in the case of x, being a rebel is a reason for giving him honorable burial, but in the case of y, being a rebel is a reason for denying him that honor. Cf. Wiggins (2006), pp. 277–280, where he argues on Aristotelian grounds for a position close to what Dancy calls particularism.

    Particularism has not gone unchallenged. See Crisp (2007) and Väyrynen (2006) for examples of strategies against Dancy's position.

2. In Sophocles' *Philoctetes*, Odysseus is represented as an unprincipled teacher to a young man; the audience would surely have identified him with teachers of the new learning such as Protagoras. On such teachers' alleged relativism, see Bett (1989).

3. Stafford 2003, p. 49.

4. In Homer's *Iliad* Book 1, Agamemnon refuses to give up his trophy woman, for the good of the army, unless he is compensated by the gift of Achilles' trophy. The consequence is the wrath of Achilles, which brings his army to the edge of defeat.

5. Hesiod brings out the importance of persuasive ability in the kings who, as judges, must bring peace (*Theogony* 80–103). For a translation, see Gagarin and Woodruff (1995), pp. 19–20.

6. For ancient uses of contract theory as an argument against conventional justice, see Plato, *Gorgias* 483a7–484c3, in the speech of Callicles, and *Republic* 2, 358e3–359b5.

7. For fairness and the limits of fairness, see "Fairness" and "The Fairness Trap," in part IV.

The Contest:
What Went Wrong

It is a hard case. The contributions made by Ajax and Odysseus cannot be measured against each other. A throwing contest goes to the quarterback, a shoving contest to the offensive lineman. Any contest you propose begs the question. The team needs both kinds of contributions. How can the king determine which one deserves the greater reward? And how can he do it in a way that keeps both men loyal to the team?

At least five things are wrong in the story as we heard it. Each one deserves a chapter in its own right, but here is an overview.

First failure—the big overall failure—justice failed to serve its purpose

The purpose of justice is to maintain the integrity of a community—to resolve disagreements within a community in such a way that the community survives. In this case (let us assume) the Greek army truly had achieved the right outcome: the most valuable player got the award. But the right outcome was not enough. The army came apart and lost its second most valuable player. The army needed to go beyond the right outcome to something else—a deeper kind of justice, justice in the very souls of the people.

Second, this story brought justice into conflict with compassion

Maybe that does not bother you, but it should. Justice and compassion are too important for us to let either one be sacrificed to the other. Many thinkers see justice and compassion as doomed to be in conflict.[1] They are deceived by appearances. The true conflict, as we shall see, is between justice and fairness. Fairness is about principles; justice must treat principles with great caution. The real things, real justice and real compassion—these cannot come into conflict because, in the last analysis, they amount to the same thing: wisdom.

Third, the army is poorly led

In fact, the army is organized in a way that invites suspicion about any decision that is made in it. Such an army can only play at justice, and never in a way that is wholly convincing. At the heart of this group of men is not justice but command.

The army is a tyranny. Agamemnon and his brother have the authority to manipulate whatever procedures they set up. Ajax cannot have confidence in the fairness of anything that the commanders do. The army therefore fails to meet a necessary condition for long-term survival as a community. We know this from the rage of Achilles, which nearly tore the army apart, according to the *Iliad*, long before the Ajax contest went wrong. The army is not working as a community; therefore, it does not have any shared virtues as a community. Most important, the army cannot believe itself to be a just and decent society. For that belief, its soldiers would need to be confident in the quality of their leadership.

Agamemnon, however, does not know how to be a leader. Agamemnon tries to rule through instilling fear, but a leader would rule through commanding everyone's respect and by setting an example for subordinate leaders. To nurture mutual respect, a leader gives respect to those who follow; and to set examples, leaders cultivate good character in themselves. They show that they are moved not by self-interest but by the larger values and goals of the group. And in doing any of these things, leaders use wisdom.

Suppose the Greek army at Troy did make that correction. Imagine that the army serves a state that inspires trust, one in which there are no tyrants because all leaders are subject to the rule of law. And suppose that this army has a leader who is wise. Would that be enough for Ajax? Perhaps it would, if the army could have decided against him in a way that inspires trust. But in the story as we have it, that condition is not met.

Fourth, the procedure aimed at fairness but produced only discontent

The procedure Agamemnon followed could not be trusted by both sides. He chose a procedure that made Ajax feel the contest had been fixed. The real contest was between brains and brawn, but Agamemnon transformed this into a contest of speeches—and that is just brains against brains. That decided the issue before the judges had a chance. Everyone knew Odysseus had the better brain. Ajax was right to be furious. Odysseus would have been equally furious if Agamemnon had proposed that the two men have a tug-of-war. That would have thrown the contest to Ajax. But a fair contest would not throw the issue either way.

Suppose we had to choose between a spelling bee champion and a math whiz for our top academic prize. Would it be fair to settle the matter with a spelling bee? No, we need a procedure that both sides can agree is fair. Here's a procedure for Ajax and Odysseus, which was used in some versions of our story:

Capture a dozen Trojan prisoners and ask them who posed the greater threat. The prisoners say the greater threat came from Odysseus. They say they could see Ajax wherever he was on the field of battle, but Odysseus's tricks could hit them where they least expected. Asking the prisoners looks like a better procedure; at least it is less likely to be fixed one way or the other. But this too would fail to mollify Ajax.

Ajax would be even angrier than before, if the procedure were one in which he had decided to trust. He would be even more hurt if a plainly fair procedure were public, as it would be if the commanders made the proceedings transparent to the larger community, as fairness seems to require. Consider a simple modification to the original procedure. Instead of inviting the two contestants to speak, arrange for military experts to testify on both sides, and leave the decision to the jury. So long as the experts are chosen in an impartial way, this looks fair. But it will not produce the desired result. The more fairness we put into the procedure, the greater the insult to the loser, who will learn by this method that his peers think poorly of him. Fairness is a trap, as we shall see.

The more reasons you give him to believe that the decision was made in accordance with fairness, the more deeply he will be insulted. How dare they disrespect his strength and loyalty, whoever they are? Every time you tell him the decision was fair, you are telling him once more that he was found inferior. You are destroying the foundation on which his life and his honor have been built. Everything he has done for the Greek army he has done because he believed that they all knew he was the strongest, the bravest, the most loyal—in short the best—of them all. His belief in himself cannot let him accept this story about fair procedure.

In order to save his self-respect, he will have to convince himself that he was stabbed in the back. He believes that Odysseus could carry off a trick like that—to make a false trial look fair—and Agamemnon would have been his accessory. Justice is supposed to heal the wounds of a disagreement. But fairness does not promote healing.

Fifth is a failure of character

The winner and loser both need to have justice in their hearts and souls, but nothing in this story took their hearts into account. A bad loser will be angry no matter what the outcome turns out to be. A bad winner could have spoiled the result by gloating in a way that would dishonor the loser. To see why this matters, we need to remind ourselves what rewards are for. They express the values of the community by conveying honor where honor is due according to those values. And their goal is to support, not undermine, the fellow feeling of the community.

When a reward is given, it should be given in a way that allows others to be pleased at two thoughts: first, they should be pleased to see justice in action when they see that good work has been given its due; and, second, they should be pleased at the thought that they too are eligible for recognition. If Odysseus were a bad winner he would have emphasized his singularity and refused to admit that others contributed to his success. In the shadow of a bad winner we have no cause to rejoice, no reason to hope for ourselves.

Odysseus appears to be a good winner in Sophocles' version and in mine, but Ajax looks like a horribly bad loser. If he were a better loser, would the dilemma go away? Don't count on it.

Notes

1. "Justice does not include mercy, but is opposed to it" (Lucas [1966], p. 234). Lucas follows an ancient tradition. Plato has Socrates decline to appeal to the pity of his judges, arguing that justice forbids it. Apart from the fact that such behavior would shame the city, he says, "I believe that justice forbids one to plead with a judge nor to be let off after pleading [so as to be pitied to an extreme, (*hina hoti malista eleêtheiê*)]; rather, one should inform the judge and persuade him (*didáskein kai peíthein*)" (*Apology* 35b, with bracketed context from 34c).

PART FOUR

Justice as Human Wisdom

Few hurts which human beings can sustain are greater, and none wound more, than when that on which they habitually and with full assurance relied fails them in the hour of need; few wrongs are greater than this mere withholding of a good; none excite more resentment either in the person suffering or in a sympathetic spectator.

—J. S. MILL, *Utilitarianism*

| Bad Losers

The sickness of lusting after justice.

—WILLIAM STAFFORD, *Every War Has Two Losers*

Ajax is a colossally bad loser. Deprived of the reward he believes he deserves, he runs amok and tries to kill both his commander and his rival for the reward. His anger is as huge as his body, but this may not be a bad thing. In his mind, his anger is no larger than the insult he has received. That is one reason that Odysseus feels compassion for him. As do we, the readers.

You lose your grip on justice if you care about it too much. Justice is a matter of poise and balance. In the end, it is a kind of human wisdom. Wisdom is like a skittish kitten that runs away when you try to grasp it in your arms. Ajax is like a young child, trying to control a pet that will not accept control. Justice is of paramount importance, don't get me wrong. But if Ajax truly had justice in his mind, he would not lust after it as he does. Justice makes people good losers.

Bad losers come in several flavors, all of them failures of justice. Here is a short catalogue:

Insufficient Anger, or Anger Too Late

Anger is a good thing. Without it, Ajax would be a doormat. In fact, Ajax has been deficient in anger for nine years of warfare. He is far too loyal and long-suffering. He has given more and risked more than any other soldier, day after day, without any special recognition or reward. When he does realize that the commanders have been taking him for granted, thinking of him as a dumb ox easily goaded into service, then he snaps, and all the anger he has not been feeling at the conscious level surges to the surface and overflows.

Ajax is a bad loser not because he snaps in the end; he is a bad loser because he has been losing all along and has not done anything about it. Instead, he has been accepting his losses quietly, so that no one knows his potential for anger. The commanders continue to take advantage of him, with no awareness of the dangers that lie ahead. A wiser commander would have foreseen Ajax's anger years before the surge; but in this army's command team no one is wise.

Good losers know when to be angry.

Too Much Anger, or Anger Misdirected

Anger can be too quick and too fierce. So it was in the case of Achilles, whose famous wrath rose and fell with the plotline of Homer's *Iliad*. Achilles' anger at Agamemnon was justified. Agamemnon had been a peevish, selfish, irresponsible commander; more tyrant than leader, he has a terrible record of driving subordinates into destructive rage. But Achilles' anger was out of proportion. It hurt his own friends more than it hurt Agamemnon.

Ajax, who treasured friendship, made the point simply in his visit to the sulking Achilles. After the more polished speakers had made their elegant points, Ajax simply said, in effect, "We are your friends, and you have abandoned us." That was enough to bring Achilles partway back onto the team. At least after that he no longer planned to set sail for home.

When the time comes for anger, good losers focus their anger on the person who has done them wrong—not on the wider community. And their anger is in proportion to the insults they have received.

Good losers are angry enough, but no more.

Ignorance about Others

Part of Ajax's anger comes from another source: he is angry because the reward went to Odysseus, whose contribution means nothing to Ajax. As a man of action, Ajax (like many ancient Greeks) despises words and everything that exists at the level of words. Odysseus is a master of words and of the stratagems that can be developed in words, so Ajax despises Odysseus. That attitude caused no harm so long as Odysseus received no special rewards. But now that Odysseus's word power is recognized, Ajax is angry. He thinks, "That big bag of words, how many lives has he saved on the battlefield? All he does is pull the wool over the commanders' eyes. How could they be so stupid as to reward a soldier for mere words, empty words?"

Any team calls for contributions of different kinds. In a healthy company that is innovative, the marketing folks and the creative types recognize the importance of their very different kinds of work. In the world of sports, everyone on a healthy team appreciates the contributions each member makes. In a healthy philosophy department, the historians appreciate the proofs of the logicians, while the analytic metaphysicians appreciate the teaching of the practical ethicists. But philosophy departments are less likely than sports teams to be healthy in this way; they have less need for health. The same goes for many kinds of institutions that manage to survive without teamwork.

Good losers understand the value of everyone's contributions.

Self-Deception

Ajax has been right about himself all along. He has truly been making the strongest contribution on the field of battle day after day. But many losers are self-deceived. They think they are doing very fine work indeed, and they are aggrieved to find that others do not agree. They feel that they must have been stabbed in the back by some secret enemy. They know who the enemy is, and in their hearts they harbor a passion for revenge.

One might feel, "The boss hates people with my hair color, or my politics, or my sense of humor. And look, the others do too! I have lots of enemies! They are all against me. They form a conspiracy to defraud me of my recognition. Otherwise, how could it be that no one recognizes the fine work that I am doing?"

Sometimes self-ignorant bad losers falsely attribute their troubles to prejudice over race or gender or sexual orientation, and then there is hell to pay. Sad to say, such charges are true, all too often. Good losers ought to complain when they are victims of prejudice, but the self-deceived complainers give good losers a bad name when they protest against prejudice. They set back the cause.

The self-deceived bad loser is a tough challenge for leadership. Leaders who try to lead self-ignorant losers out of their self-deception are likely to encounter irruptions of anger. Before trying this, a wise leader would consider whether the underlying cause in a given case is really self-deception or a difference in the kind of contribution that the loser has made. If the loser is doing something well, the wise leader rewards that, hoping to see more action along those good lines. But if the loser is doing nothing well that the group needs, then the wise leader should somehow send the loser away. No doubt the loser will make an exit complaining of a stab in the back to all who will listen, but no one is likely to listen to this song for very long.

Good losers know just how good they are.

The Tender Ego

Some losers are winners but do not realize it. Their egos are so tender that they take the slightest setbacks as major losses. One might say, "I may be recognized as one of the most productive scholars in my department, but no one seems to listen to me in meetings. So I speak more loudly and more often, and the others pay even less attention to what I say. The only plausible explanation for their refusal to listen to me—a leading member of the department—is a conspiracy against me."

This is a variant on self-deception. Tender egos are not deceived about the quality of their work, but they are wrong about what they are entitled to on the basis of that work. The best scholar may rightly be outvoted again and again on issues of policy. The best marketer may rightly be ignored on basic design decisions. The best quarterback does not have the power of the coach. The best actor does not direct the play. But tender egos may be deceived on that: "If they really recognize that I am the best actor, why don't they listen when I suggest some business for the other lead? Plainly, I am not appreciated here and I should look for another company."

The tender ego is a serious challenge for the wise leader. Too good to fire, too touchy to get along with the others, tender egos require special handling, and sometimes they are worth it.

Good winners know they should not win all the time.

Managers Who Insist on Winning All the Time

Bad managers (who are not leaders) set bad examples by refusing to lose. A manager or commander who is a bad loser breeds trouble. If you have any of the faults listed earlier, you will not be a leader: if you do not know when to be angry, if your anger is out of proportion, if you are not able to appreciate the different values that support your teams, if you are ignorant about the quality of your own work, or if you have a tender ego that insists on winning every contest.

Leadership is about setting an example. On any team, there will be losers, and every leader will have to sustain some losses. For example, the team may have good reasons for trashing a plan that the leader has cherished—a defeat for the leader, but a victory for the entire team.

A manager who sets a bad example should not be surprised to find that others follow that example. Leaders know when to lose gracefully, when to give others credit, and when to make use of talents of others that they do not have. They know when to be angry and when to be calm.

Leaders are good losers.

Insensitivity

Most competitions have at least one winner. You lost, but one of your colleagues won. Now you, as an insensitive loser, have one trump card to play: you can spoil the day for the winner.

If you are sensitive, however, you will not do this. Joy in the workplace is too scarce a commodity to squander in this way. A good loser has the capacity to appreciate the winner's feelings and will not try to kill the joy of winning. The good loser does not need to share the winner's joy. That is asking a lot after a grievous disappointment. But you can appreciate and support the winner's joy without feeling it yourself. The ability to do that is compassion.

Compassion is equally important in a good winner. Good winners need not share the pain of losers, but they need to respect that pain and they should do nothing to exacerbate it.

Good losers—like good winners—are compassionate.

Compassion

> "Can we not convict and yet mitigate the penalty?" asked the sailing master here speaking, and falteringly, for the first time.
>
> "Gentlemen, were that clearly lawful for us under the circumstances, consider the consequences of such clemency.... Your clement sentence they would account pusillanimous. They would think that we flinch, that we are afraid of them—afraid of practicing a lawful rigor singularly demanded at this juncture lest it should provoke new troubles."
>
> —HERMAN MELVILLE, *Billy Budd, Sailor*[1]

Fearing mutiny, Captain Vere reminds his court that law aboard a man-of-war must be as brutal as war itself. And so Captain Vere rejects compassion; he refuses to consider the state of mind or intent of the accused. For all that, in peacetime he would allow law to make finer discriminations than he believes can be safely entertained for sailors in combat readiness.

Some thinkers have argued that compassion and justice are fundamentally at odds.[2] But we need to distinguish among three things: clemency, pity, and compassion. Pity is the feeling we have for any condemned prisoner, if we are sensitive enough.

Even when we believe the prisoner is guilty and deserves the penalty, we can feel pity. But that need not lead to clemency. Clemency would result in softening or canceling the sentence. We might be moved to clemency simply out of pity, but that would be foolish. If we are to choose clemency, we would be wiser to do so under the influence of compassion, which I take to be a kind of understanding.

Compassion is the ability to understand the feelings of another, without necessarily sharing them. In the case of Billy Budd, the captain has enough compassion to understand Billy's heart. Billy Budd is good at heart, through and through, as the captain knows. Although Billy has caused a man's death, he is, in a deep sense, as innocent as a man could be. The captain's compassion tells him that the penalty he exacts on Billy Budd would be wrong in normal circumstances. Compassion ought to allow for a fine adjustment of penalties to the degree of wickedness displayed by the accused— in other words, compassion ought to allow for justice, in this case for giving Billy what is his due.

The captain, however, believes that compassionate justice would not be safe aboard a ship at war. He fears that the common sailors would not distinguish between compassionate justice and pusillanimity, or cowardice on his part. But there is danger of a more subtle confusion, between pity and compassion. Pity is not discriminating in the way that compassion is; were he moved by pity, the captain might abstain from the death penalty altogether. A decent heart could feel pity for any criminal on the threshold of punishment. If the crew believes that Vere is easily moved by pity, they may conclude that the captain will put all punishment in abeyance. But compassion does not put punishment in abeyance.

It informs justice—it provides the understanding that will allow a judge to give accused people what is due to each of them.

Pity would abrogate justice, where compassion would make justice more perfect, by fitting the penalty to the state of mind of the accused. If the captain were to decide for clemency, he would have to make it clear he was doing so for the sake of justice, not out of pity or even simply because he has compassion. Justice is giving each person what is due to that person. The presence of compassion could be misleading. The crew needs to understand that what is at work in the ship is justice, and that they should each expect to get what is their due from Captain Vere. The captain fears that the crew will not grasp the distinction between weak-minded pity and compassionate justice. If Vere had decided for clemency, his decision would in fact have been informed by compassion, but not driven by it. He is probably right in believing that his crew would not have understood the distinction.

Tecmessa has this right. Tecmessa and Odysseus both feel compassion and use it, but they do so in different ways. Out of compassion, Odysseus holds back from jeering at Ajax. "I could be in the same position," he says in Sophocles' play. In this case, compassion works irrationally, like pity, trumping any reasons that might be advanced for taking the opposite course. His compassion directly prevents him from jeering at Ajax.

Tecmessa cannot say that she could find herself in Ajax's situation, since she is not a soldier. Her compassion rises from another source—from her ability to recognize the feelings of others. Because of her compassion, she understands Ajax's feelings, along with the feelings of the commanders, and therefore she is able to grasp two essential facts: the commanders will not be moved by compassion, and Ajax would be insulted by it. Her compassion teaches her to tread softly where soldiers' honor is concerned. And so she does. She urges the commanders to realize that it is in their interests to save Ajax, and she sees that Ajax can be saved only if he is persuaded that the commanders truly recognize his value to the army—as a matter of justice. She is a deeper moral thinker than Odysseus.

The difference between Odysseus and Tecmessa is about how they respond to compassion. When Odysseus sees Ajax in his rage, compassion simply holds him back from action. When Tecmessa advises the commanders, she takes compassion as a teacher that helps her understand that only justice—and not compassion—may be considered a reason for giving her husband the armor. In other words, Tecmessa's compassion does not lead directly to action, and Odysseus's compassion does. But her compassion affects her thinking about how she should act; it colors the reasons she thinks must be considered in deciding the case.

This is a subtle point. Compassion (in my version of the story) makes Odysseus feel like turning the armor over to Ajax. With her more complex reasoning process, Tecmessa can see that compassion would be a reason for not doing this, because it would make Ajax feel even worse. Ajax wants honor, not compassion. If the prize is an expression of compassion, it is an insult.

A rule of thumb for justice: insofar as justice aims at maintaining a sense of community, it cannot simply follow compassion. And it should not give compassion as a public reason for a decision. But justice should always consider what compassion tells us in a given case. The better you understand the feelings of those involved, the more likely you are to find a solution that heals the community—a solution that is recognized as giving people what is due to them.

Compassion of Tecmessa's kind has much to teach about justice because it helps us understand the feelings of the members of the community—feelings that a good judgment strives to bring into harmony. A compassionate judge understands the feelings on both sides of an issue.

Some philosophers have held, as a principle of justice, that justice must ignore compassion, because compassion leads to mercy; such thinkers take mercy to be invariably a breach of justice, because mercy undermines principle. This is going too far. Judgment on the basis of principle ought to be undermined, as Aristotle pointed out, because particular cases vary too widely for one principle to yield justice every time.[3]

Compassion will have a role in restoring justice when it alerts the judges to notice how poorly a principle or a rule or a law applies to the case at hand. What we want from justice is a sustained sense that our community is giving all the members what is due to them. Sometimes a law leads to a result that shatters that sense in a particular case. Suppose a boy kills his abusive father. Then we might say: "Yes, I know the law says he should be executed or shut away for life for the crime against his father, but look, his father was abusing him violently and sexually. Knowing that, we cannot infer from this action that the boy is a danger to society. We need to know more before we condemn him. Shouldn't the law take this into account?" But the law does not always show so fine a grain.

Compassion teaches what an officer of the law should consider in a particular case, even when the officer knows that the law in general cannot consider such things for all cases. The law on the books is not at fault; Aristotle would say that the trouble is in the particular circumstances of our lives, which do not lend themselves to being generalized about.

Compassion in Tecmessa helps her appreciate the nature and the depth of Ajax's feelings. Her compassion enables her to understand that acting out of compassion would scrub salt in his wounds. Compassion cannot be the reason for giving Ajax the armor; if it were the reason, then justice would fail, and the prize would carry no honor. Instead, it would bear a stigma. Tecmessa understands that. In doing so, she recognizes the difference between understanding through compassion (which seems right in many cases) and acting simply on the basis of compassion (which would often be unjust). The case nicely illustrates the point at which compassion should affect the outcome.

I insisted at the start that compassion and justice must be compatible, and so they are. But I must now enter this caveat: being compassionate and acting from compassion are not the same thing. The doer of justice may be compassionate, and in some case *must* be compassionate in order to appreciate the feelings of those involved and give them their due. But the doer of justice in most cases may not use compassion as the sole reason for action: she does not say simply, "Compassion makes me soften the penalty," but, with more sophistication, "Compassion helps me understand why he did this, and with that in view I consider his action to be a lesser crime than first appeared; therefore I am deciding for a lesser penalty."

How, then, does Odysseus persuade the commanders to permit Ajax to be buried? The law of tradition says Ajax should be left unburied for the dogs and the carrion birds to tear apart. Recall the crime: Ajax attempted to murder his commanders. The penalty for such a crime is death without burial. Ajax is dead already, so the remaining issue is burial.

Odysseus's argument to Agamemnon (as I render it) is built on the particular facts. Ajax is no ordinary would-be assassin. He was honor-driven to his crime by what he perceived as an enormous insult from Agamemnon, whom he had loyally served through nine years of battle. "This could be you or I," Odysseus says, meaning not that you or I could turn assassin at the drop of a helmet, but that you or I could be so angered by an inept king that we would feel like restoring honor through violence.

In calling these circumstances to mind, Odysseus is thinking like Tecmessa. He argues for sparing Ajax on the basis of his realization that Ajax's case is highly unusual, that the extraordinary passions driving him have an origin we can all understand through compassion, and that a man in the grip of such passions is not fully responsible for his actions. Indeed, the king who provoked him can be held accountable.[4] The point is not that any of us could succumb to a berserk rage—but that Ajax's special circumstances help us understand his anger as anomalous. It is not only that his responsibility is diminished by his madness, but also that his situation is so unusual that it is unlikely to serve as a bad example to the other troops.

To hold his army together, Agamemnon must steer between two dangers. If he veers left toward the reef of compassion and starts making decisions simply out of compassion, simply because he is sorry for the offender in each case, he would wreck the army. The troops would no longer believe that each one is likely to receive what is due, if compassion keeps intervening on sound judgment.

On the other hand, if Agamemnon veers to the right, he will crash into the tall straight cliff of the law. A decision made simply from law—not to bury Ajax—would leave the army with a powerful sense of injustice. Ajax would not be getting his due.

Odysseus has it right this time: he would not want to serve a general who would leave his greatest hero unburied, and neither would the other soldiers, who realize that they are all Ajaxes—that an insult to Ajax is an insult to all who serve loyally. The army would melt away if Ajax were left unburied. The middle way—the only way to victory—is justice informed by compassion.[5]

Compassion versus Law

Laws often come into conflict with compassion. That is the theme of one of Shakespeare's more mysterious plays, *Measure for Measure*. A good-hearted ruler has found that his leniency has led to lawless debauchery. So he takes a sabbatical, leaving his power in the hands of Angelo, a man known for his puritanical strictness. At the center of the play is a scene in which a lovely young woman pleads with Angelo for the life of her brother. The word she uses is "mercy."

"Mercy" is ambiguous, veering between compassion, pity, and clemency. When Isabella pleads with Angelo for mercy, she is actually pleading for the compassionate justice that would lead to clemency. Her brother has broken the law, albeit in special circumstances. He has slept with a woman who is not his wife, but she is his fiancée, and the wedding has been wrongly delayed. Anyone so situated would find it hard not to break this law. But Angelo is adamant:

> *Angelo:* It is the law, not I condemn your brother.
> Were he my kinsman, brother, or my son,
> It should be thus with him: he must die tomorrow.
> *Isabella:* ... Go to your bosom,
> Knock there, and ask your heart what it doth know
> That's like my brother's fault. If it confess
> A natural guiltiness such as his,
> Let it not sound a thought upon your tongue
> Against my brother's life. (Act 2, Scene 2)

Compassion is understanding another person's feelings, and this is what Isabella wants from Angelo. Compassion is not the same as pity, and it is not the same as clemency. Pity can operate without understanding. Clemency—letting an offender off the hook—could be a consequence of either pity or of compassion; it could be foolish, if caused by pity, or wise, if arising from compassion. But Isabella is not asking Angelo to be foolish. She is asking him to understand, on the basis of his own emotional history. She is not asking him for empathy as this is often understood; she is not asking him to share her brother's feelings. Compassion may, however, be understood as the capacity for what I have elsewhere called "cognitive empathy.")[6]

What compassion tells us is no use unless we are prepared to make exceptions to rules or laws. Exceptions are a tricky subject because they can lead to a breakdown of order, as Angelo has reason to fear. The enforcement of law has been pitiful in his state for some time, both ways—pitifully weak and swayed by unthinking pity. As a result, order in the state has collapsed, and Angelo is responsible for restoring it. Even so, we in the audience are on Isabella's side.

The law in Ajax's case is that rebels who threaten the life of a king should be stoned to death and left unburied. Even if we think that the law is right for most cases, Odysseus would persuade us that it would be unjust to enforce this on Ajax. So he has persuaded Agamemnon, and us, to allow an exception to the rule.

Every ethical thinker stumbles over tough examples. Homicide is wrong, but what about self-defense? Self-defense is permitted, but what about defending yourself against an attack that you yourself provoked? That's not permitted, because the provocation was not permitted in the first place. But maybe self-defense in such a case should be permitted if the other guy was going to go gunning for you anyway, and you had to provoke an attack so that you could be justified in getting him out of the way. Is that permitted? Already the case (which is not uncommon, especially in warfare) has become so complicated that we don't know where we stand. The rules may not always help us—not unless we bring good sense and a strong moral compass to applying them.[7]

The ancient Greeks held that only human beings were capable of compassion. Their gods lacked a moral compass, and, to make matters more frightening for us humans, the gods of Greek myth had no capacity to put themselves in the shoes of a suffering, erring human being. The Christian tradition is opposite on both counts. In a famous scene in Shakespeare's *Merchant of Venice*, Portia gives mercy a divine status, above what she calls the "force of temporal power":

> But Mercy is above this sceptred sway,
> It is enthroned in the hearts of kings,
> It is an attribute of God himself;

> And earthly power doth show likest God's
> When mercy seasons justice. (Act 4, Scene 1)

The trouble is that when mercy seasons justice, justice no longer appears to be fair. People who commit the same crime may not pay the same price. And people who achieve the same goals may not receive the same reward. That is not fair.

Notes

1. Melville left the manuscript of *Billy Budd* unfinished in various drafts. I have taken all quotations from the text by Hayford and Sealts (1962), which makes the implausible claim to be definitive.
2. See p. 88, n. 1.
3. Aristotle, *Nicomachean Ethics*, bk. 5, chap. 10, where he says that what he calls equity (*to epieikes*) yields results with more justice in them than universal laws could yield. Equity and compassion are not the same thing, because equity can be a reason for a certain judgment and compassion cannot; compassion can be a guide to where equity lies.
4. Aristotle points out that actions taken in a passion of anger may be unjust, but they are not evidence that the character of the agent is unjust or wicked (*Nicomachean Ethics*, bk. 5, chap. 8). "For the one who started it is not the one who acted from anger, but the one who provoked that anger" (1135b26–27). In some cases, the bad character is found in the person at whom the anger is rightly directed. Odysseus in the *Ajax* rightly says: "Insults are understandable / When a man has been insulted himself" (1322–1323).
5. On the complexities of forgiveness, see Griswold (2007). On the ancient Greek attitude to compassion, see Konstan (2001).
6. See Woodruff 2008, pp. 181–182.
7. On the need to make exceptions: philosophers have adopted various strategies. Some try to devise rules that cover all the hard cases; others hold that no rules can hold without exception; still others argue that rules hold under certain conditions. This group uses Latin expressions like *ceteris*

paribus, *pro tanto*, *prima facie* for the way these rules hold. These are fancy ways of saying that the rules hold most of the time, without specifying where they do not hold. On these issues, see especially Dancy's elegant analysis of alternatives (2004), pp. 118–139. My view, based on Plato's theory, is that we must keep our eye fixed on unchanging moral ideals, such as justice, which are never precisely instantiated in our messy world. See my "Platonic Virtue," forthcoming.

| Fairness

The fundamental idea in the concept of justice is that of fairness.
—JOHN RAWLS[1]

Imagine the story this way. Before the contest, Ajax and Odysseus agree on a procedure for deciding who gets the armor. They will collect a bunch of newly captured Trojan prisoners and ask them which of the two heroes frightened them the most. The prisoners will vote, and their vote will be final. Since both candidates have agreed in advance to the procedure, neither one can have any ground for complaint. Everyone will have to accept that the decision is fair.

Fairness looks like a safe refuge for those who practice it. If Nestor could prove that the decision had been fair, he would be doing the king a great favor. Who could complain about a fair decision? Well, Ajax may complain about any decision he does not like, Nestor admits, but that just proves how crazy Ajax is. Fairness, Nestor believes, should always come out on top. So let's give fairness a chance.

Fairness seems to have three main features: equality, agreement, and transparency. The first two are mainstays of most modern theories of fairness. The third, transparency, is something employees insist on when they ask for fairness in rewards.[2]

Equality is the first goal of fairness. If possible, fairness treats everyone the same way. In the Ajax case, equality is beyond reach. For one thing, even if the two contestants are judged equal, we have only one suit of armor to hand out. For another, even if we had two suits of armor, we could not give the same prize to both candidates. That is because each one of them wants to have the honor of being recognized as the best soldier in the army. There can be only one top honor—only one best soldier, only one highest salary, only one corner office. Once the question is asked that way, we will have to settle for inequality.

Agreement, the second goal, comes in when equality fails. When we can't dole things out equally, but if we still want to be fair, then we are asked to follow rules or procedures that everyone has agreed to—or at least ones that everyone *would* agree to, if everyone were reasonable. When fairness rules, it makes us unequal only in ways that we would all agree to, under certain conditions. We will see that this is the hard part—working out what kind of agreement would put a glow of fairness on inequality.

The transparency of fairness allows anyone to predict accurately what results to expect. No one is surprised. If a bonus is linked by a formula to performance, then everyone knows what bonus to expect from a certain performance. That is fair. The problem with transparency is that it may set up a trap for management. What are we to do when performance is so creative, so original, so successful in unpredictable ways that it does not fit the formula that was announced in advance?

Equality and Its Discontents

The glory of fairness is that if two cases are alike—if two employees are equally productive—then fairness gives them equal rewards. The difficulty is that two people are rarely exactly alike in what they do, so that fairness often puts people into groups and treats everyone in the group the same way—and that may not seem right for everyone. A better solution is to go for proportional equality: the ratio of your reward to mine should be equal to the ratio of your productivity to mine. If you produce twice as much as I do, you have earned twice the reward. That seems fair.

Real life, however, is often too messy to allow equality to rule even under a proportional system. People are hired at different times, under different agreements, and inequality results. Often this is due to what is called salary compression: people who were hired earlier, at lower salaries, don't catch up with people hired more recently, under reward policies that treat both groups equally or proportionally.

The Ajax dilemma points to another complication: people do different kinds of work. Accounting is not the same as design, and making the product is not commensurable with either marketing or design: none of the three makes any money by itself, so there is no common coin by which we could measure which is the most valuable. In the world of Ajax, leading an infantry charge is not the same as devising a clever strategy, and yet victory will not come to the army unless it has good people in both areas.

Victory will not come unless the best people are retained. Rewards look to the future as well as to the past. Salary is supposed to pay for what workers have actually done; rewards often aim to retain people with a view to what they will do. We know that Ajax's contribution will not win the war for us, but we can only surmise that Odysseus will come up with a strategy that will. If Ajax wins the prize, he will win for what he has done; if Odysseus wins, he will win for what we hope he will do. Past and future are not measured in the same coins.

So fairness needs to go beyond simple equality. It has to adopt a fair way of making decisions in matters like these. The usual solution for rewards in business is to let the labor market decide. That is rather like letting the Trojan prisoners decide the Ajax case. If there is more competition for accountants than for designers, the market would give them higher rewards. In the academic job market, economists are paid far better than classical scholars—not because anyone judges them to make a more valuable contribution to the university but because the business world provides a second market for economists. We will ask whether such a result meets the second standard for fairness: Would agreement make it fair to let the market decide?

Trying to Agree

A fair way of making decisions is one that everyone concerned can agree to. That is easier said than done. Rarely will all members of a unit agree on anything that affects their status as individuals. So fairness takes a detour through a thought experiment: it adopts principles and procedures that everyone would accept if they were all reasonable. Of course, we are not all reasonable, and none of us is reasonable all the time. So this part of fairness depends on philosophy, or, rather, on a story made up by philosophers.

The experiment is a story that runs like this. Suppose a group of people met to discuss what would count as fairness. And suppose they had certain things in common: they care about what is good for them and for each other (which means they must share some basic ideas about what is good for people); and they must be willing to compromise; they must also be willing to reciprocate—to give in return for receiving. You can expand the premise of the story in several directions, but at some point you have to draw conclusions: these principles and these procedures are fair because we could (in the fiction of this story) all agree to them. Of course, this result is based on a story we made up, but we can defend the story on the basis of theories about what it is to be reasonable on such matters. This is agreement in a thought experiment.

Making Inequality Fair

Here is one principle that has resulted from a story of this kind. Reasonable people would agree that they will accept inequality only if the people who get the worst deal out of it get a better deal than they would have had overall if everything were equal.[3]

Consider Ajax. Suppose that we have reason to expect that Odysseus will be hired away by the Trojans; we know he puts himself first and will work for the highest bidder. If we do not give him the armor of Achilles, we stand to lose Odysseus. If we lose Odysseus, we lose the war. If we lose the war, we all lose our investment in it, and none of us gets a share of the booty. Now,

Ajax is due a large share of the booty if we win; let's say his share is worth ten times as much as Achilles' armor. So Ajax is better off overall if the armor goes to Odysseus.

Arguments of this kind are given to justify the salaries and rewards that go to upper management. We all get stock options, so if we keep talented leadership aboard, even at a high cost to the rest of us in diminished salaries and rewards, we all do better overall. But there's a catch. The argument assumes that "better off" means just one thing—carrying off more booty, or making more money. In real life, we find that people's concerns about salary level are not just about money. They are about what money signifies, which is far more important than money to most of us—recognition, respect, honor, and status in the group.

Ajax is especially devoted to honor. The armor is worth nothing else to him. It is too small to wear, it loses value if he melts it down for the precious metals in it, and there is no market in which he could sell it. All it means to him is honor—a recognition of his exemplary service in the army, his long-suffering loyalty to his friends, his courage, and his magnificent strength. Odysseus has never cared about honor; all he cares about is winning and going home, by whatever means he can. So this argument does not work for Ajax. He wants what is due to him, and he wants it far more than he wants to win the war and carry off his share of the booty.

So the thought experiment fails in this case. So does the Trojan prisoner gambit, and for the same reason. Ajax wants the honor that is due to him, and he would never agree that a bunch of frightened Trojan prisoners are any authority on that. Agamemnon and the other people whose lives he has saved—he wants them to be the ones who recognize the level of his deserving. As for the labor market, which is analogous to the prisoners' verdict, no reasonable person would agree that the market will give people what they truly deserve. We accept the market's verdict as brute fact. If only financial well-being were at stake, we would be able to defend the labor market by means of our thought experiment, if we could show that the losers are better off as a result of the market than they would be otherwise. But rewards are not merely about money. Honor is at stake.

Now for the really hard question. May we say that Ajax is irrational in putting honor ahead of profit? By what right could we say this? The Ajax dilemma shows that we can have irreducible conflicts over what is good, and that these conflicts undermine any attempt to make inequalities look fair. Similar conflicts undermine attempts to adopt a fair procedure for decision making. We have already seen that any procedure we devise for solving the Ajax dilemma is unfair. A contest of words is biased toward Odysseus, a tug-of-war toward Ajax. That is because the two contestants contribute different kinds of value to the common cause, and there is no fair way of measuring the contribution of one against the other. As we have seen, their contributions are incommensurable.

One problem about fairness, then, is that it may simply not be possible. But let's suppose it is possible for the moment. Can you achieve fairness without laying a trap for yourself?

Fairness and Exceptions

Suppose you have agreed with your employees that you should not give everyone the same bonus, and you proceed to set up a procedure for determining the size of each bonus, according to rules that are published and known to all. Your Bonus Board has met and given you its recommendation, based on the rules, as to how the bonus fund should be parceled out.

Then you find that Odysseus is being courted by the Bank of Troy, which is offering him a juicy package to come over to its side and devise stratagems for profitable derivatives that will help it steal a substantial part of your business. Now you decide that you need to set aside the recommendations of the Bonus Board, so that you can give Odysseus a bonus large enough to keep him working for the Bank of Achaea—a decision that cannot be squared with the published rules.

Let's suppose, further, that you believe your decision is so clearly in the interests of all that, if asked, the reasonable employees would agree to this exception to the general rule. Some, however, perhaps a majority, will be offended and do their best to thwart your decision. They may have the moral high ground; after all, Odysseus's stratagems may be winners, but many employees believe that such stratagems should not be adopted by an honorable banking company.

You do not dare hold an open discussion of the issue. For one thing, you don't have time for a lengthy debate, and you fear, in any case, that the debate itself would seal Odysseus's decision to go over to the Bank of Troy. Even if you were able to keep him, a public discussion of THIV, his Trojan Horse Investment Vehicle, would make the vehicle useless.

So you satisfy the agreement condition in a thought experiment: "Suppose we were all reasonable; then we would agree to my making my decision this way." Now you have done what fairness requires except for one vital thing: you have violated transparency. You had to do that to keep Odysseus.

You offer him the bonus, with good results, and dole out smaller bonuses to the other employees than fairness would require. They rightly complain that you have not kept your word, and that you have not been fair, even though they are all better off by your decision. The Bank of Achaea thrives, and the Bank of Troy soon goes under, its assets gleefully plundered by the very troops who complained about your decision. Perhaps you would have been wiser never to promise fairness in the first place, but simply to ask for the trust of your employees to handle bonuses in the way that is best for all. You would have done better to stay out of the fairness trap.

Notes

1. This famous claim was first published in John Rawls, "Justice as Fairness," *Journal of Philosophy* 54 (1957): 653–662. His theory was elaborated over the course of his career in inspiringly humane ways. For a readable account, see Pogge (2007). In what follows I make no pretense to giving a full account of Rawls's theory, which is far richer than this brief treatment could possibly show. In particular, I do not bring out Rawls's own interest in good character.

   Rawls and his followers own only part of the concept of fairness—the part that deals in a principled way with basic issues of social and political justice. The Ajax dilemma is not concerned with such basic issues as concern a nation-state, or society as a whole, or the larger community of rational beings. Rather, the Ajax case focuses on the kinds of issues that arise in relatively small communities—academic departments, football teams, families, small businesses. The same conceptual apparatus belongs to both arenas, but pragmatic considerations are more evident in the smaller ones.

Most English speakers apparently do not distinguish between justice and fairness; hence scholars who work from empirical studies treat the words as synonyms, for example, Sheppard et al. (1992), p. 3.

2. While philosophers over the last half-century have generally followed Rawls in their treatment of fairness, management experts have taken an approach based on empirical research into what employees count as fairness, for example Sheppard et al. (1992), Folger and Cropanzano (1998). There are excellent reasons for the empirical approach: employees who feel they are unfairly treated are likely to do something about it.

3. This is a simplified version of John Rawls's difference principle (above, note 1).

| The Fairness Trap

Moral arrogance involves holding that your moral decision or judgment is the only correct decision or judgment on a controversial topic when there are conflicting moral decisions or judgments that are also morally acceptable.

—BERNARD GERT, *"Moral Arrogance and Moral Theories"*

Fairness is a trap because once you commit yourself to it you must submit to it.[1] You are no longer in control because you have waived the right to exercise good judgment. Fairness is like a machine into which you put the facts; then out comes a result, which is predictable by all concerned, and which you could not change without creating an annoying sense that you are unfair.

If you committed yourself to a fair procedure for dividing the bonus pool, you have lost control of the situation. Your fairness wore a spurious air of objectivity; you have simply pushed the subjective element in your choices out of sight—back to where you chose the procedure or chose the people who chose the procedure, or back to the imaginary place where your thought experiment played out. You pretended to be on the "royal road" that would attain justice, but there is no such road, and you should not be surprised to find that you have failed to accommodate all of the interests involved and the passions they set afire.[2]

You might stand by your fairness and try to be happy with what it brings. In doing so, like Agamemnon at the start of our story, you might make Odysseus and many other soldiers happy for a short time—until you learn how angry your fairness made Ajax, and the army begins to come apart in shreds of rage. Or you might have subjectively adopted a procedure that would give the prize to Ajax with an appearance of objectivity. That would make him and his friends happy for a while, until they all learn that Odysseus has now been bought by the Trojans, and the Achaean army is soon to be defeated by his stratagems. Your fairness could generate either result and leave either a toxic residue of anger or a legacy of defeat.

"Tough," says Fairness (if we can give it a voice); "that is what ethics requires." If Fairness were always right, then the ethical leader will go down to defeat. Ethics and success would part ways. But Fairness is not always right. Ethics does not always require it. Sometimes, fairness is right and suffices for justice. Sometimes it is on the right track but needs justice to bring it home. Sometimes, however, justice and fairness conflict, and then justice is the better choice.

Justice versus Fairness

Fairness is the double of justice; that is, fairness looks like justice, but it isn't the same.[3] Here are a few marks of the difference:

- Justice is an ideal goal; fairness is fairly easy to achieve in practice.
- Justice requires judgment and leadership; fairness is content with adherence to rules.
- Justice has a place in the soul; fairness, at best, has a place in the mind.
- Justice aims to prevent or relieve anger; fairness often exacerbates it.
- Justice considers the whole health of a community, aiming to give all members a sense of inclusion; fairness focuses on individuals.
- Justice never insults or humiliates, but a fair distribution of goods could be humiliating to some recipients.

Imagine a school lunch program designed to ensure that poor children receive nutrition equal to that of others, but carried out in such a way that some poor children are humiliated at every lunch hour. That would be fair enough but not just.

Justice should soothe the savage breast, but we are so constituted that fairness can exacerbate differences and make the breast more savage. The price of fairness can be high; fairness is compatible with insults and humiliation. Honors and insults rub off on larger groups. Insult Ajax, and you insult the common soldiers. Insult a black professor, and you insult her race. Honor her, and you honor the race. Fairness cannot take this into account because it tries to overlook factors such as race and gender.

In the interest of fairness, the military during the Vietnam era rotated individual soldiers in and out of the combat zone and in and out of combat units. This aimed at fairness among individuals:

most ground soldiers served the same number of days at roughly equal levels of risk. But this rotation scheme destroyed a sense of inclusion in communities.[4] In this case, sad to say, fairness destroyed justice. It took individuals into account only as individuals, with a sad result: at the end of a tour they were left as shards of a fractured community. But justice looks to the bonds of a community, to a sense of belonging. Fairness at this level gave returning veterans a harder time fitting into life outside combat than they would have had if they had stayed within their units.

The Fairness Zone

For all its faults, fairness has a zone where it must be zealously preserved. The worst clashes between fairness and justice occur in marshy areas around the zone, where reasonable people disagree as to whether fairness or justice should win.

Equal pay for equal work lies at the center of the fairness zone. The principle concerns pay, and not rewards in our sense. It also assumes equal work, and therefore it cannot be applied to Ajax and Odysseus, since they do different kinds of work. But many sorts of work allow rough judgments of equality, and here the principle comes into its own. Differences of race or gender or religion or sexual orientation are irrelevant to the measure of equal work, so that fairness must not take them into account.

There is no good reason for justice to consider such differences either. Unless, well, unless what? Other differences could throw the decision into the marshes: Andrea is rich and single, loves the nonprofit cause for which she works, and wants to work for a pittance to save the cause's money. Pierre is penniless. He loves the same cause and wants to work for it, but he cannot do so on Andrea's wages because he has a family to support, children and an invalid wife.

In such a case, does a wise manager force Andrea to take the higher wage, equal to what Pierre needs? Pay them differently for similar work? Or sadly release Pierre to serve in the corporate world at higher pay? You might ask Andrea for her view of the matter, but you will probably not get an entirely true answer, as Andrea's view is not clear to herself. "Sure, pay Pierre more than you pay me," she will say, but later she may find herself resentful at being asked to work as hard as he for less than he is paid. Her intentions are good, but if poorly paid she may unconsciously set a lower value on her work than on personal affairs and so drift into bad work habits. So Andrea and Pierre are still in the fairness zone, where most issues of salary reside.

Rewards are another matter. Promotions are rewards, if not based routinely on time in grade. So are merit scholarships, and so are admissions to elite schools and colleges. In such cases we tend to take outcomes as evidence of fairness: if 55 percent of those entering a large firm as associates are women, we would expect that the same should be true of those promoted to be partners. If not, we may reasonably infer that the promotion system has not given the candidates what was due to them—unless we are given a different explanation for the discrepancy.

Admission to elite universities is a reward of an especially sensitive kind, as it affects both individuals and the groups to which they belong. Transparent race-based admissions processes meet criteria of fairness, in my view, but they have proved to be socially divisive. Some people believe that college admissions belongs in the fairness zone; others see this as belonging to the larger and more difficult region where conflicts of interest between groups must be accommodated.

The solution in recent years has been to push admissions processes into the shadows. One way is to admit students on the basis of transparent criteria that are obscurely linked to race—such as class rank in a population of schools that are de facto segregated by race. Another way is to use multiple criteria for what is called a "holistic judgment." Both ways achieve a just outcome by working in shadows that are incompatible with perfect fairness, because they are not fully transparent. The admissions offices have found that when they work toward justice across ethnic difference, full transparency causes a political backlash and can land them in legal difficulties. Shadows can serve good purposes.

When one group is more successful in rewards than another, justice is at stake. The less successful group will suspect prejudice and chafe against it. Their anger may grow to rival Ajax's anger. If so, it will tear at the fabric of the community. This is a matter of justice. Unlike fairness, justice lives in an area where actions that affect the status of a group work also to honor or to insult members of that group. Here honor and insult loom larger than profit and loss because they spread through groups, while profit and loss go only to individuals.

Justice requires that the honor of groups and their members be addressed. One way to do this is to adjust criteria for promotion or admission in such a way as to achieve a just outcome, so that no group appears to be at a disadvantage. But this solution seems to violate fairness; some members of the group that had formerly enjoyed an advantage will cry foul, claiming that they are not being treated fairly as individuals. A school might accept lower test scores for admitting applicants who are scored high on what is called an adversity index (largely a measure of poverty). This is not an insult to the children of the rich, but it does give their less affluent competitors a lower hurdle than the one they have to surmount.

Affirmative action is a good example of an issue that is swamped in the soggy boundary between the zone of fairness and the world of justice. The acrimony on both sides is fed by living streams, justice on the one side and fairness on the other. I offer no cure for the acrimony here; we have good reasons for caring on both sides.

Fairness Beyond Its Zone

Fairness is often a source of pain. That is one reason it often deflects justice from its goal of sustaining harmony. Even rational losers do not want to hear that they lost by a fair decision. They generally prefer to believe a different story.

"What? You lost your job?" I will not comfort you if I go on to say, "I am so sorry, but the decision against you was entirely fair." And I would not expect you to say that you performed poorly and were selected for downsizing by a fair process. What I expect to hear is along these lines: you had an enemy in high places, you were stabbed in the back by someone you considered a friend, or you were the victim of stupidity in management circles. Anything but admit to a fair loss.

If you believe in betrayal or conspiracy or managerial stupidity, then you—the disappointed candidate—come off well. Good people are often cheated out of what they deserve. It is easy to believe you were betrayed; it is much harder to believe that you are not good enough to win in a fair contest.

How do you tell your friends that a decision has gone against them? I have been a department chair, and I have had to tell people that they would not get tenure. Often, in such a case, they wanted to believe that they have been betrayed; someone had it in for them; the process was unfair, a conspiracy.

I was young then. I knew that a process could deliver the wrong outcome and still have been fair. I believed the process had been fair in all of these cases, and I thought I should show my friends that this was true: they had not been betrayed; the process had been as fair as could be expected; the committees at each level simply had not been persuaded by the evidence we had provided. To my surprise, my arguments made everyone angrier than ever.

Twenty years ago I received a letter from a senior colleague raking me over the coals for the way I handled merit raises (a kind of reward). I was then a very young chair in my department. Eager to be fair, I had arranged to canvass each member of the department separately to ask them each who they thought most deserved one of the few raises I was in a position to give, on the basis of teaching, service, and recent publications. Each person gave me a short list, and the lists more or less agreed. Moreover, I had asked the dean to put the money slated for my raise into the general pot, so that I would get none and no one could accuse me of feathering my own nest. What could be fairer than that?

Everyone had a voice, everyone was heard; the criteria were clear and the method transparent, except that each individual's list was not public. Moreover, the decider had nothing to gain or lose.

I should have expected it: my colleague was furious when I told him no one thought he deserved a raise, and that he would get none. He had not published in years but pulled down one of our largest salaries. "I happen to believe I am pretty smart," he told me. I agreed. I thought he was the most intelligent member of the department, and I knew that he used his intelligence to our benefit both in our meetings and in his teaching. He was brilliant at coaching graduate students and younger colleagues (such as me) in academic writing. I realize now that my fairness insulted him. He wanted me to recognize the unique contribution he made to the department, and he hated my way of hiding behind the judgments of my peers. His letter accused me of bad faith. In effect he was saying: "You have the authority to decide these things. Why are you afraid to say what you think?"

Maybe he thought if we had it out between us, and if I did not seek shelter behind our colleagues, that he could browbeat me into submission. But I think better of him than that. He was asking me to treat him with respect, to acknowledge his uniqueness and the distinctive value of his contribution. Instead I had marshaled the opinion of the department against him.

Fairness does not in itself support morale, and insisting on fairness may damage it, as in this case. Should we therefore abandon fairness altogether? Surely not. Blatant *un*fairness would be even more damaging than high-visibility fairness. The Ajax dilemma is, after all, a dilemma—something we can survive one way or another but not solve.

Fairness in elections is as painful as fairness in the giving of rewards, but unfairness in elections is far more damaging. After an election we often hear the losing side claiming unfairness. They cannot believe they lost a fair race. "We were robbed," "The voters were brainwashed," "The other party wickedly caused voter fraud on a large scale," or "The other party wickedly disqualified thousands of voters in key areas." We in our party are sure we would have won a fair election, because we are in the right. And so we feel this election could not have been fair. Otherwise, the good guys would not have lost.

Proving the election fair does not heal the rift, but proving it unfair would widen the rift still further. If it was not fair this year, we must make it fair next year, or risk the kind of disaffection that can fatally divide a nation. In elections, the transparency of the process is especially important: the public should have reason to believe that, for the most part, all and only legitimate votes are counted.

For the giving of rewards, the case is different. Transparency in the process threatens the privacy of the people involved and can exacerbate the pain of a loss. Transparency may provide traction for a lawsuit, as managers in our litigious society are well aware. Transparency of criteria may work against the success of the community; if the criteria for rewards are clearly stated, they will be limited by the imaginations of management, with the result that they may either be unjust to Odysseus or stifle innovation altogether.

What to do better? Fairness alone does not help with rewards, and an insistent, transparent fairness makes things worse. Only a few rewards are available (or they would not truly be rewards); yet we must try to recognize the different ways in which members can be of value to our team, and we must try to do this without insulting those who lose out. For this we will need good winners, good losers, and wise leadership at all levels. That is a long way of saying that fairness is not enough; we need justice.

Notes

1   Thanks to Reuben McDaniel for the expression, "the fairness trap."

2. "Justice, I think, is the tolerable accommodation of the conflicting interests of society, and I don't believe there is any royal road to attain such accommodations concretely." Judge Learned Hand, quoted in Philip Hamburger (1946), pp. 122 and 125.

3. Justice, during the last half century, has been treated as fairness by most philosophers, under the influence of John Rawls. In this small book I do not launch a full critique of Rawls; I simply present an alternative account, based on classical models. See p. 160, n. 10, for a brief review of major critical arguments against Rawls.

4. Such is my own experience. On the effect of this more generally, see Jonathan Shay (1994), p. 198: "Unit rotation is the most important measure for secondary prevention of combat PTSD [posttraumatic stress syndrome]." This has been tested in more recent wars. See Hovland (2010) for a recommendation that National Guard troops returning from combat zones be kept together longer than is currently the case in order to identify and mitigate cases of PTSD. Hovland is a colonel in the National Guard.

Good Things and Their Doubles

Laches: So I think courage is a certain steadfastness[1] of soul…

Socrates: I expect that you consider courage to be one of the really good things.

Laches: Yes, of course; one of the best.

Socrates: So is steadfastness fine and good if it comes with good sense?

Laches: Yes, very.

Socrates: What if it comes with foolishness? Isn't that the opposite, harmful and bad?

Laches: Yes.

Socrates: So would you call such a thing good, when it is harmful and bad?

Laches: That wouldn't be right, Socrates.

Socrates: Then you agree: That sort of steadfastness is not courage, since it is not good, and courage is good.

—PLATO, *Laches* 192b–d

aches is an Athenian general with enough combat experience that he ought to know what courage is. He does know something about courage—enough that, when questioned by

Socrates, he can come to see that his initial definition was wrong. Steadfastness is not courage. It just looked that way to him when he started to talk. The difference between them becomes obvious when he realizes that steadfastness is not always a good thing. It can be foolish. Real courage, by contrast, is never foolish. And this he believes.

For similar reasons, I have argued that fairness is not justice; it only looks that way. Justice makes room for compassion, in order for justice to be reliably good. But fairness cannot do that, and so fairness cannot always be good. Let us agree that justice is one of the finest goods that human beings can seek. But fairness, as we have seen, does not look good to us in cases that call for compassion. So they are not the same.

Courage and Its Double

A really good thing—an ideal—usually has a double that is not so good. Courage is a good thing. One of its doubles is fearlessness; fearlessness is attractive and easy to understand, but it is not a good thing. Fears save your life every day; without fear you might step in front of a car, put your finger in a light socket, set sail in a hurricane, or take heroin of unknown strength. You would be a fool to wipe out your capacity for fear. You may think it would be ridiculous for a courageous person to be subject to fear, but then you would be confused by a double. Fearlessness is not courage; it only looks that way.

Doubles are misleading. Fearlessness looks so much like courage that when I ask people what courage is, they often answer that courage is not being afraid. Of course, even young children retract that answer as soon as they are asked to think what would happen if they really were without fear in a dangerous situation. Luckily, fearlessness is so obviously a bad thing that we can easily cure the confusion this double causes. Still, we need to see why fearlessness is so attractive, and why it looks so much like the thing it isn't—like courage.

Courage (I propose) is the ability to persist in doing the right thing in the face of fear or the possibility of fear. Fearlessness is not having fears to face. Let's suppose these definitions are true. Are they clear enough to be helpful? Our definition of fearlessness gives us a sharp criterion: you are fearless if you do not feel fear, and we know what that means because we can easily identify fear. But our definition of courage does not give a criterion with sharp edges because all too often we do not know what the right thing is. Is it right for the senator to vote against a good bill for fear of losing the next election, if doing so will allow for many good votes in the future? Our definition of courage does not give us the answer. Our account of fearlessness applies, however: the senator would be moved by fear. But is that really cowardly? Not if he is doing the right thing.

These definitions allow us to see the difference between courage and its double. Once we see that, we see why a definition of courage as an ideal will not *by itself* help us on the road to courage; all it does is help us stay off the wrong road. The road to courage lies not in definitions, and not in criteria. Like all the most important roads, it heads for the high ground of human wisdom.

My definition of fearlessness, by contrast, points to a road that does not challenge us to scale great mental heights. All you have to aim at is to stop having fears. That is easier said than done, but we know what it means, and we know some ways of doing it—drugs, drink, mental damage, or behavioral conditioning. Now we see why fearlessness is so attractive; unlike courage, it is not a mystery. And at first sight fearlessness does look as if it would make you stronger. It won't, of course; it will sooner make you dead.

Doubles have this general feature: they are attractive because they are easy to define. But because they are easy to define, they are not really good things. We cannot rely on them to be what we want. As a general rule, if we hear a clear and usable definition of a good thing, we are in danger of being taken in by a double. If all the good things were easy to define, we would find it easy to live a good life. But we don't.

The fearless person will always go into any danger without qualms; but the courageous person will respond differently to different dangers. The courageous person is aware of many possible fears and discriminates among them—the fear of pain, the fear of death, the fear of shame, the fear of doing wrong. The fearless soldier storms the machine-gun nest no matter what; the courageous one may decide to go around it or even to retreat, if that is the right thing to do. It takes courage to retreat in good order, and double courage to retreat when you are afraid that others will try to make you ashamed for doing so.

The good life would be easy if we could rely on something like courage to be unchanging in two ways—always to call for the same sorts of action, and always to be good. But our world of choices is so complicated that nothing seems to be unchanging in both ways together. If we grasp something that always calls for the same sort of action (as fearlessness does), then we cannot rely on it to be good. And if we reach for something that is always good (such as courage), then we cannot rely on it always to call for the same sort of action.

By "really good thing" I mean something we can rely on in this second way, something that is always good no matter what, such as courage or justice. Really good things are ideals; they are hard to define and even harder to bring into our lives. They are difficult because they are mysterious. We don't have a recipe or a formula for achieving the really good things. In the end they all seem to come down to wisdom. But don't give up because of that.

Wisdom and Its Doubles

Wisdom is challenging, but it is not beyond our reach. That is why I use "*human* wisdom" for what we are looking for. Human wisdom is never complete and is easily lost or mislaid when times are hard. It depends on continual personal reflection and discussion with others. These two, reflection and discussion, are essential because they can alert us to the possibility of error. Human wisdom is always on the lookout for its own deficiencies. Because wisdom is a really good thing, it has attractive doubles—so attractive that our education industry aims only at the doubles, knowledge and skill.

Knowledge and skills are easy to impart and to measure by means of standardized tests. For each type of knowledge, we have criteria, which students must meet, or else their teachers will be punished. Knowledge and skill are not as bad as fearlessness, but they are not really good things. We all know highly learned people who are fools. Experts often use their knowledge or skill to do dreadful things. The really good thing in this set is wisdom, which could guide you in using your skill or knowledge, but wisdom is hard to define.

Wisdom is the ability to make good decisions in demanding circumstances. We have no tests to measure wisdom, because we have no criteria for good decisions. Yet what we want in leaders is not knowledge but wisdom. A wise leader can make use of other people's knowledge, but managers who know so much they think they can act without wisdom are a menace.

Still, because we know how to teach and measure knowledge, we make knowledge the focus of our schools and universities. Outcomes-based assessment for all subjects is now required for accreditation in colleges and universities. We can meet the new rules when we teach skills and facts, but I do not think we know how to apply the new rules to the opportunities we give students to grow in wisdom. Skills and facts, then, narrowly defined, are becoming our goals as teachers. Education should aim higher.

Reverence and Its Doubles

Reverence is, with justice, one of the two fundamental social virtues in the ancient Greek system. Reverence leads us to feel the weakness of human beings in contrast to the majesty and perfection of the divine.[2] For this reason, reverence is the foundation of compassion, which grows from a felt sense of shared human weakness. If reverence is an ideal, then we should expect to find its doubles in common use. And they are. Being religious or being pious seems to be a matter of following specific rules of behavior or taking part correctly in certain rituals. But we find plenty of examples of people who do those things who are not reverent. Reverence is holding in awe a reality, such as God, that deserves to be held in awe. But, as prophets have been pointing out since the time of Amos, ceremony and rule-following are not suitable objects for reverence. They are ways of expressing reverence. A huge gap opens between using specified behaviors to express reverence for God, and showing reverence directly to those same behaviors in preference to God.

> I hate, I spurn your pilgrim-feasts;
> > I will not delight in your sacred ceremonies.
> When you present your sacrifices and offerings
> > I will not accept them,
> nor look at the buffaloes of your shared offerings.
> Spare me the sound of your songs;
> I cannot endure the music of your lutes.
> Let justice roll on like a river
> and righteousness like an ever-flowing stream.[3]

Nothing human deserves reverence.

Leadership and Its Doubles

If wisdom is an ideal, then so is leadership. Leadership is not the same as having power over other people. Power over other people can derive from many different sorts of things. A famous way of having power over others is by making them afraid of you. Another way is to make them love you. Neither one of these ways is leadership. The power of leadership grows from good qualities of a leader, such as wisdom, courage, justice, compassion, and reverence. Of these, the most important is wisdom because it lies behind all the others.

If wisdom has doubles, then so does leadership. The best-known double for leadership is management, defined as the knowledge or skill of getting people to carry out your wishes. Defined in this way, management is as good as your wishes. If you know what is best, your management skills will produce good results; if you are wrong, they can be disastrous. So management is not a really good thing. Management can be content with fairness, although that might well lead into a trap. But leadership aims at justice.

Justice and Its Double

Justice is an ideal, and fairness is its double. If justice is an ideal, it can't ever be bad. But fairness, as we saw earlier, can be bad. Moreover, if justice is an ideal, it should not exclude other good things, and it certainly should not exclude compassion. Yet we saw that compassion appears to be excluded by fairness, because fairness stumbles over making exceptions in particular cases.

A Table of Ideals and Their Doubles

The following table shows roughly the pattern formed by good things and their doubles. Ideals are good in themselves, but do not provide useful guidance. Doubles may be all right when guided or limited by ideals, but pursued on their own they are often disastrous.

Ideals	*Their Doubles*
Wisdom	Knowledge
Leadership	Management
Courage	Fearlessness
Compassion	Pity
Reverence	Religiosity
Justice	Fairness

Ideals are pursued through:	*Doubles are pursued through*:
Reflection	Principles
Dialogue	Algorithms
Rewards	Incentives
Shared goals	Assigned targets
Inspiration	Desires and fears

Notes

1. He means that courage is not to be deterred; it is imperturbable, not moved by fear or other considerations once it has set a course.
2. For a defense of this account of reverence, see Woodruff (2001).
3. Book of Amos (*New English Bible*), 5.21–24.

Justice

Who shall decide between these appeals to conflicting principles of justice? Justice has in this case two sides to it, which it is impossible to bring into harmony, and the two disputants have chosen opposite sides.

—JOHN STUART MILL, *Utilitarianism*

If justice is to be informed by compassion, it cannot be locked into principles. Mill backed away from principles by appealing to a broad standard of social utility—what would promote the greatest happiness for the largest number. Mill's critics attacked him for this. If you abandon principled decision making, if you become literally unprincipled, what kind of justice could you hold on to? Mill gave a powerful answer, but the language of principle still dominates discussions of justice. How could there be justice without principle?

Many recent philosophers of justice have built on John Rawls's concept of justice as fairness.[1] Fairness (as defined by Rawls) is based on principles, and principles (as Rawls understands them) are based on reason. Fairness would keep people in harmony only if they—the people—were rational enough to accept fair solutions. But real human beings are not rational enough for that.

Justice for the real world must pay due respect to all that makes up a human being.

Justice must give Ajax his due, and Ajax is not perfectly rational. He cares too much about honor to be perfectly rational. If justice is to give Ajax his due, it must give the nonrational what is due to it. Justice must pay attention to the factors that govern human behavior, whether they are rational or not. That is Plato's great insight.[2] The main nonrational factors that drive human behavior fall in two groups: those to do with big emotions, and those to do with desires.

Plato identified the chief members of the emotional group as the love of honor, the fear of shame, and anger. Among the powerful desires are hungers for food, sex, and drink, along with the yearning for wealth and the things that wealth can buy. Plato's view was that emotion and desire must be brought into harmony with themselves and with each other, and this can be done only if both are subordinate to a reasoning agent that takes their welfare into account. That, in a nutshell, is Plato's psychological account of justice. If Ajax had Plato's justice in his soul, he would have regulated his anger better from start to finish.

Plato's account of justice is on the right track. It is sketchy, however, and the sketch is illustrated only in an impossibly ideal state, one that none of us would wish to inhabit. Plato gives us little guidance on how to operate in the real world. But he does specify what justice is supposed to achieve in the real world, and that is undeniably good—peace—peace within the soul of a citizen, and peace within the community itself.

No one, least of all Plato, has a formula for achieving this goal. We have no straightforward principle to follow, which would lead us right no matter what. That is why, in a society aiming at justice, we need to have continuing discussions about how we are to form a just society. And because no one knows precisely how to do this, we cannot simply turn the task over to experts. Democratic institutions cannot be relied upon to achieve justice, but democracy at least allows for the discussion we need. We must all engage in discussing the problem of justice.

Justice as a Problem

Justice is the virtue that sustains community, as the ancient Greeks believed. The threats against community are conflicts such as feuds and civil war, and these threats are nourished by the gnawing sense that members of the community are not getting what is due to them. To sustain community, then, justice must aim at giving all members their due and, at the same time, making it plausible enough that most members believe they are getting their due.

The goal of justice is pragmatic. Justice is a virtue of individuals and communities that prevents civil war.[3] Of course, a dictator or oligarchy can prevent civil war without any recourse to justice, as millions of oppressed people can attest. When a society fractures from within, we know that justice has failed somewhere. We may not know whose injustice is to blame. Perhaps the whole society failed, or perhaps a group of its members have gone off the rails, or perhaps the failure is due entirely to an absence of leadership.

When a community does not fracture, we do not know whether it is held together by justice or by repression, or by some combination of the two. If we find what is missing in a failed society, then we have found something necessary for justice. But if we point out factors that are present in cohesive societies, we are no closer to a full theory of justice. In other words, we can know with some certainty how we could fail at justice, but we cannot know for sure—and therefore we must continue to discuss and debate—what would make our society more just. A philosopher would say that we can identify necessary conditions for justice without making progress on sufficient conditions.

At least two conditions are necessary for justice:

a. Dueness condition. Justice obtains only when each individual, and each group, has what is due to them.[4] Dueness is hard to specify, but it is plainly absent in the society that is held together by repression. Dueness is necessary, but not sufficient, because we can imagine a society coming apart even when everyone is getting what is due. In the Ajax example, dueness may well be satisfied. But Ajax is not satisfied. So we need to add—

b. Subjectivity condition.[5] Justice obtains only when people feel they are generally getting their due. Otherwise, a society could satisfy the dueness condition and still fail to meet the pragmatic goal. Not all societies that meet the subjectivity condition are just. A society that is culturally repressive may fail the dueness condition (e.g., by denying certain opportunities to women) and still meet the subjectivity condition (by persuading the women that those opportunities are not their due).

What citizens want from practical justice is a continuing sense that their community is giving everyone what is due to them. Plato writes much about the culture of his ideal city because he worries deeply about bringing people to the sense that justice is being done in it. After Plato, however, philosophers of justice have tended to set cultural factors aside. Their many disagreements about justice concern the first condition: What really *is* due to each citizen? How is that to be determined? And how delivered? This is the ongoing problem of justice. Because it is an ongoing problem, we have politics in just societies—that is, we have arenas for discussion, debate and decision, and then for revision of decisions. Nothing would be more unjust than to pretend that justice is not a problem. Justice will always be a problem.

Negotiating the Problem of Justice

Justice does three things. It sustains community by according to each member what is due to that person, and by making its decisions credible. This understanding of justice was alive early in ancient Greek culture; it is given voice by the most ancient poets.[6]

Bringing these three points into line cannot be easy. All three call for explanation. The first—sustaining community—calls for a sort of harmony but not for general agreement or consonance.[7] Justice is compatible with there being fissures opening between factions, so long as these are not so deep as to lead to civil war. And it is compatible with Ajax's being a sore loser, so long as he does not turn to sabotage (killing the generals) or defection (killing himself).

The dueness condition seems to call for fairness, but we shall see that it does not. The rewards that are due to a person are largely a matter of honor, and these must be accorded with respect to individual differences. Fairness treats like cases alike; but there cannot be much alikeness in the arena of honor: if you see only the sameness in two people, and if you therefore treat them the same, you will not do honor to either one.

Subjectivity has been neglected by philosophers after Plato: How is a community to sustain the *belief* that justice, on the whole, is being done? Those who make decisions must be credible, and all members must have the qualities that a fairly harmonious consensus requires. Members must be able to appreciate each other's unique abilities and contributions, and they must not care so much about their own passions that they are blind to the needs of the society and the deserving of others. Do not demand, however, that the members be rational. Ajax is not rational. Neither, dear reader, are you.

Justice has to take the nonrational into account in order to be credible. However well people are educated, they are subject to passions. Especially disruptive of community are the nonrational passions that arise from people's love of honor and fear of shame. Witness the high incidence of civil strife in academic departments among scholars who are widely read and widely published. No one who has chaired an academic department would believe that higher education leads to rational behavior in a community.

There is no simple algorithm for sustaining justice—no straightforward way to measure what is due to any particular member. Each human being is different from every other, and each makes a unique contribution to the whole. To make matters more difficult, not all the contributions are commensurable. Someone must make hard decisions. Many people will dislike the decisions, but someone—ideally the one who made them—must have the ability to convince people that the decisions are a fair approximation of justice.

A leader decides well, communicates well, and is trusted. A just society needs leaders.

Incommensurability

If Ajax and Odysseus were doing the same kind of work, and contributing the same kind of value to the joint effort of the army, we could appeal to a simple principle: equal rewards for equal work—or else rewards proportional to the quality or amount of the work. But the Ajax dilemma is not so easily solved because the two contestants work along different scales of value.

Odysseus makes plans; Ajax does the heavy lifting. Both are essential. But there is this difference: Odysseus can present his contribution as unique: no one but he will dream up the Trojan Horse or any of the other stratagems that will win the war. If he sold out to the Trojans, the Greeks would lose the war. So the Greeks must at all costs keep Odysseus on their team.

So it is with Odysseus's children in our own time: the finance whiz who dreams up more profitable derivatives—our bank must pay him enough to keep him away from rival banks. Or take the top-ten epistemologist who would raise the standing of any philosophy department simply by moving there. He can bargain his salary beyond the range of a Supreme Court justice, while the academic children of Ajax—the heroic teachers who manage heavy loads without tenure—are paid at roughly the rate of lawn-care workers.

We are told that such inequality is the effect of the market on labor, and that we should therefore accept it as justice. But we can bring forward no principles of justice to back this up. If the children of Ajax form a union, they may have the power to change the situation; otherwise, the children of Odysseus will continue to have the power to increase the gap. This story is not about justice through markets; it is about the exercise of power through the labor market.

Labor market results are not (or not merely) an expression of power; they express the values of the society that creates the markets. If early childhood teachers are paid less than college professors, this represents two facts: more people can qualify for one job than the other, and society sets a higher value on one job than the other. If society set a higher value on nursery school teachers, it would raise the entrance qualifications for the job, reducing the number of eligible workers, and then, through the market, increasing their salaries. But nothing in this story speaks credibly of justice. The market does not give people what we believe is due to them. Most people, for example, do not believe there is justice in the bonuses going to whizzes in finance. The labor market fails the credibility test.[8]

Value and Procedure

Justice must consider the relative values of the things we do. That is hard, and procedures do not help, not by themselves. The weakness of procedural accounts of justice is that they are value neutral. But justice cannot be neutral about value.

The underlying problem between Ajax and Odysseus is this: a fair resolution of the rewards issue would require us to determine which one made the more valuable contribution. But there is no single scale of value for making such a determination. Any procedure you design to determine their relative values will either beg the question or yield a result that will not have the confidence of all concerned. Understand the question this way: Could there be a procedure for distributing rewards in which Ajax and Odysseus could have equal confidence? Apparently not.

Suppose you summon a panel of Trojan prisoners and ask, "Who frightens you more?" And they ask back, "What do you mean—on the field of battle, or over the long term?" The question you ask changes their answer. If you say "over the long term," that throws the contest to Odysseus; if you say "on the field of battle," Ajax is the clear winner. So justice requires us to ask the right question in this procedure. But how are we to know what is the right question for this case? The procedure proposed here gives no guidance on that. We would need another procedure to determine what question to ask.

If we keep asking, we will be running down a regress to infinity. Suppose you propose a procedure for choosing the question to ask— say a panel selected by lot from the army. How will we determine what question to ask the panel that is convened to determine what question to ask? This could go on forever. Forever, that is, unless we know at the outset what values justice calls us to promote in our distribution of rewards. If we find that loyalty is the highest good for a soldier, Ajax wins. If we find it is cleverness, Odysseus. And so on.

Suppose we convene a jury of Greek soldiers and give Ajax and Odysseus equally smooth-talking attorneys to represent them.

"Who is the most valuable soldier?" asks the judge. "What do you mean by 'valuable'?" asks the jury. If the judge gave an answer, that would bias the outcome. But suppose the judge does not give an answer: "You decide," says the judge. The jury hammers out an answer and presents it. But there is nothing in this procedure (qua procedure) to give the people confidence that the panel has got the relative values right in accordance with justice.

Generally, we do not expect juries to make judgments of value, but judgments of fact, under law. Similarly, tenure committees are not asked to judge whether teaching or research is of greater value; they are given the university's public standards for tenure, and they judge on that basis, regardless of their personal values.

Now let's try a famous gambit proposed by John Rawls, the most distinguished philosopher of justice in the previous century. Suppose we imagine two rational, well-intentioned people who, in ideal circumstances, are supposed to agree on principles of fairness. And suppose they know that one of them might well be an Ajax and the other an Odysseus, or vice versa. They cannot know their lots in real life. Then we ask them under what circumstances it would be fair to give one of them a greater reward than the other. Rawls's proposal is that they would agree to what is called the difference principle—that it would be fair to give one of them a greater reward if the one who got the lesser award were better off as a result than he would have been had this difference not existed.

Now by the standard of wealth, Ajax is better off if Odysseus gets the armor. The booty Ajax can realize from the sack of Troy far exceeds the monetary value of the armor. If Odysseus is miffed and goes home, the army will lose the war, and none of them will win any of the booty they would pick up when they captured Troy. On the other hand, Odysseus is not better off if the armor goes to Ajax. Ajax is less likely to go home anyway, and if he does, he can easily be replaced by four ordinary men.

The weakness of this line of reasoning is that Ajax has a different scale of value: for him, the most important outcome is not wealth but the honor that is due to the value of his particular work. He is committed to a set of values by which he excels and Odysseus fails. Courage deserves honor, he believes, trickiness does not. Rewarding trickiness, he believes, is outrageously wrong, even if the trickiness is beneficial to him.

The Ajax dilemma concerns a decision over a clash of values. Principles of fairness are supposed to be neutral with respect to values. This rubs off on procedures, insofar as they are fair. Suppose our tenure decisions turn out to sustain the values that ought to animate a great university. We could preserve these values and make sure our decisions are fair in terms of procedure. But our decisions could be fair and still go wrong on values.[9]

None of the procedures I have discussed could give Ajax a reason to believe that he is less deserving of the reward than Odysseus. Suppose we draw the veil of ignorance for Ajax before he becomes Ajax and ask him what sorts of procedures would make for justice in rewards. One procedure might work better for Ajax, another for Odysseus; but none could determine the relative values of loyalty and trickiness. Justice will have to address Ajax's conviction that loyalty is honorable and trickiness dishonorable. But no procedure can, by itself, do that.

Part of the Ajax dilemma is this: justice calls for a resolution that gives Ajax his due, and, moreover, justice calls for a way to make people—including Ajax—believe that what it gives him is his due. Ajax, the living, breathing, sweating Ajax, the big man with the history of loyal self-sacrifice for friends—this Ajax, not the one who might assent to a principle from behind the veil of ignorance—this Ajax must be persuaded to let go of his quarrel with Odysseus.

That is what incommensurability means for justice in rewards. The two soldiers' contributions are incommensurate because they represent competing values, and no procedure can resolve the competition by itself in a way that sustains community. If justice can be found in this area, then, it will not be based on procedures.[10]

Experiments in Justice

If Ajax had been kept from burial, as the law required, after all that he had given to the army, the soldiers who saw themselves in Ajax would have been angry, and they could well have decided to abandon the army and go home. So Agamemnon probably did save the army by taking into account the special circumstances of the case and allowing the burial to proceed. In fact, he did that and the army did stay together.[11] But that fact alone cannot ground the claim that Agamemnon's mercy was just in this case. We would need also to show that Ajax and the other parties had their due, in order to ensure that justice was served.

Suppose, on the other hand, that Agamemnon had shown mercy and the army had not stayed together. On this scenario, many soldiers would see that the king's mercy trumped the law and would conclude that the army would lurch along without law and order for a while and then disintegrate; so they might as well cut their losses and go home now. Or they might conclude that they could safely rebel against their commanders. If this turned out to be the fact, should we conclude that justice forbids mercy in this case? No. On this scenario, the breakup of the army is due to the fact that it has been held together by threat of merciless discipline; there was no justice in this army long before the question of mercy arose.

Officers in the military have usually been merciless, especially in combat, to prevent mutiny and rebellion in the ranks. For this reason, Captain Vere decided to execute Billy Budd, who was morally innocent and deserved clemency if anyone ever did. But Billy was guilty at law of an offense that would be construed, like Ajax's, as attempted rebellion. And so he died. Captain Vere is wise enough to see that this is not justice but a consequence of the larger cruelty of war itself. And we can see that Vere's navy, composed of men and boys pressed by violence into service, was hardly a just community.

Now suppose that the army would have come apart on either decision. Burial would have emboldened one large group of soldiers to rebel, and nonburial would have offended another group so deeply that it would have gone home. Then we should say that neither of the alternatives could serve the goal of justice, owing to a sad state of affairs in the army itself. Had justice been instilled in the army from the beginning, then either decision would have worked. The army would have trusted its command team; the troops would have stayed together whether or not Ajax was buried.

In a healthy army—that is, one in which justice prevails—Ajax would have appreciated the value of Odysseus, and this story would never have taken the sad turn that led to his suicide. Again, in a healthy army, the troops would have understood Agamemnon's mercy as peculiar to Ajax's special case and would not have come apart.

But this is not a healthy army. Few people trust Agamemnon. Agamemnon has been weakening the army for years. He insulted Achilles. And when he tried to win Achilles back, Achilles did not believe that his offer was sincere.[12] In such a society, we will see many failures of unity, but none of these will point to the precise point at which justice failed. It has failed in too many places for that.

Justice cannot be settled by an empirical test for right or wrong decisions.[13] In a really healthy army, either decision would work; in a really unhealthy army, either decision would fail. By looking at empirical outcomes alone, we cannot evaluate Agamemnon's decision to extend mercy to Ajax. We need to look into the whole health of the army.

We are reduced to considering thought experiments to work out what promotes the health of the army and what destroys it. Such experiments are fairly easy in a simple case like Ajax's. In real life, the factors that would cause the army to stay together or fall apart are harder to isolate. We cannot test hypotheses about justice through social experiments. Only in thought.

Justice without Principles

No one should be surprised that my approach yields a concept of justice that is independent of principle.[14] My starting question was, after all, pragmatic: What sort of justice would have worked to keep this army together? For any principled answer we can imagine some circumstance in which we would see that the proposed principle would fail to keep the army together—while a less principled justice would succeed.

Agamemnon's method was to find what he deemed the right outcome and declare it justice no matter how it was achieved. We saw why that would not work. By one obvious standard, Odysseus is the most valuable player because he is the soldier who cannot be replaced. On this showing, the outcome was right. But neither Ajax nor any of his children would accept justice of this sort. A different standard seems more obvious to them—Ajax is the most valuable because he shows the virtues of courage and loyalty most consistently in battle, and these are the virtues prized by the army. By that standard, justice would give the prize to Ajax by any means necessary. The outcomes approach fails in two ways because it does not resolve the underlying conflict.

Nestor's solution was to find a principle of fairness he considered sound and then follow that through a fair procedure to whatever outcome it produced. Then he would declare all of that—principle, principle-governed procedure, and outcome—to be just by virtue of the fairness of the procedure. But Nestor's attempt at justice would fail. Ajax and his party would not be content with it. As we have seen, a clash of values cannot be resolved by appeal to procedure—unless, that is, we assume a high level of rationality on the part of Ajax and Odysseus. But justice must give what is due to the irrational.

The defender of principle might say, "The Ajax dilemma arises only because the main players are idiots. Why, after all, should these two soldiers quarrel at all? The booty they expect to gather after the fall of Troy will give each a share worth far more than this one suit of armor. If they shared the goal of maximizing their individual booty, and pursued that goal in a rational way, neither one would want to spend a minute on this quarrel." But of course they want the armor not because of its value as treasure but for what it means—the honor and respect that come with the armor to the soldier who wins it.

Suppose (as is not the case) that the two heroes cared only about the monetary value of the armor, and that they could agree on the monetary value of the work each does. In that case, we could resolve the conflict (says the defender of principle) by working out a proportional solution—give Odysseus the armor, for example, and Ajax a sum of money determined by this formula—Odysseus/Armor = Ajax/X, that is: the value of Odysseus's work divided by the value of the armor = the value of Ajax's work divided by the sum to be given him.

Aristotle would like this answer. He grounds his account of justice on equality and its cousin, proportionality: you and I should have equal shares if we do equal work; if not, our shares should be proportional to our work.[15] Most modern accounts of justice follow Aristotle onto the path of proportionality. That would be fine if the work that I do can be measured against the work you do. But if the two kinds of work are incommensurable, then we have no numbers to stick into the formula.[16]

To do what he does, Ajax must show up on the field of battle in full armor day after day and, if battle is joined, slog through one engagement after another, staying in the battle line where his companions need him to be. For this, Ajax needs courage and fortitude, and a sense of duty to his comrades. We can measure the time he spends on the job. We can count the times he comes to the aid of a wounded comrade and the times that other troops start to flee, but he stands fast, and the better soldiers rally around him. All these are things we can measure or count, and the results for Ajax are stupendous. We know that Ajax and his kind are essential to winning the war. Still, we also know that no number of Ajaxes can succeed in taking Troy.

Odysseus, by contrast, does not have to do any of these things to make the peculiar contribution he makes. Odysseus must do a lot of thinking. He can do that in or out of his armor, by day or by night, alone or with others. He must have the freedom to have lots of ideas—bad ideas as well as good ones—so that the best ones may rise to the top. He needs to have an untrammeled mind, but he does not have to be an especially good person. Unlike Ajax, he can succeed without physical courage (although in fact we know that he does have that). Overall, Odysseus's productivity is much harder to measure than Ajax's, and none of the things we count or measure in the case of Ajax are appropriate for an evaluation of Odysseus. Still, we know he is our best hope for winning the war.

So there is nothing to count or measure that would resolve the Ajax dilemma. Justice requires us to recognize both values, in a way that is credible to each. The trouble with fairness is that it wants to treat everyone the same, or as nearly the same as possible. But justice—if it is to serve its primary purpose of resolving disputes amicably—must pay attention to individual differences.

Consider inheritance between two children with different needs and abilities. One plays piano, the other the violin, and each hopes to inherit and to play the fine instrument that the family owns. Market forces have raised the value of the family violin far beyond that of the piano. Should the parents make up the difference in cash? Neither child has any special need for money. The market values of the instruments fluctuate, and the parents may not leave enough cash to pay for the difference. A calculator will not solve this problem.

Goodwill is essential. No judgment, however good, will resolve disputes unless the people involved have justice in their souls—the qualities of soul that help them accept a wise settlement.

Justice works without principles, but it cannot work in a moral vacuum. The society and its members must share certain virtues. And through sharing these virtues they must be capable of working out a rough consensus on how to give the members their due. The virtues that support a just society must exist both in the soul of the individual and in the culture of the community:

Justice in the individual soul (a moderate disposition with regard to anger and honor on the one hand and desire for personal satisfactions on the other).

Justice in the community (the ability to make decisions that inspire trust because they do not appear to be bent to support any special interest, under leadership that pursues common goals).

Both of these depend on other virtues, one of which stands out as especially important for the kind of justice that considers feelings and restores a sense of justice in the community:

Compassion (respect for the feelings of members of the community whose fortunes are different from our own).

Justice also calls for wise leadership. Wise leaders serve a number of purposes in justice. Their skills in communication, along with their personal credibility, will help make the community's decisions credible. And by their personal qualities they will set good examples that help sustain a culture of justice.

Leadership is a matter of ethics; where it occurs, it moves people (insofar as it is leadership) not by force or fear but by the virtues of the leaders. The virtues of leadership start with justice and compassion but include also courage and wisdom. Beyond virtue, wise leaders have the ability to display their virtues in their actions and their speech; they communicate well; they are trusted and, as a result, they build mutual respect.

No one can give a recipe for growing any of these virtues. Where justice occurs no one can pick out precisely what it is that has put it there and what it is that maintains it; I will do my best in the chapter on leadership. But we can identify factors that destroy justice easily enough. The most surprising of these is fairness.

Notes

1. For Rawls's theory, see p. 118, n. 1. While philosophers have concerned themselves with justice as an objective value, management experts have based their work on empirical studies of what people accept as justice. A table showing various approaches to justice from this point of view, with citations, is to be found at Sheppard et al. (1992), p. 43. See also Singer (1997) for a helpful survey of both traditions.

2. Plato's ideal city, developed in the *Republic*, is a thought experiment designed to bring out the truth about justice. Like most modern readers, I find the

ideal city odious in its separation of classes, its control of poetry and information, and in its single-voice approach to harmony. The theory of justice that emerges, however, deserves more attention than modern thinkers have given it, as I will argue below, p. 167.

3. *Protagoras* 322b-2; *Republic* e.g., 8, 347a: civil war starts when unqualified people become rulers.

4. The initial statement about justice in Plato's *Republic* expresses this idea, taken from the wisdom literature of the poets (Simonides): Justice is to give everyone his due (*prosêkon hekastôi apodidonai, Republic* 1, 331e3, 332c2), and the entire argument of the book can be understood as Plato's attempt to find the meaning of this.

5. The subjectivity condition is widely recognized in the management community. "What is 'actually' just, by some objective or independent standard, really matters a lot less than what is *perceived* to be just" (Sheppard et al. [1992], p. 9. "People who feel injustice do something about it" (ibid., p. 136). See also Rousseau (1995).

   This condition is also addressed in classical theories such as Plato's, which stresses the importance of using communication (especially through the arts) to develop harmony and a sense of shared justice across the community. Plato's means include censorship, which violates basic liberties—an important element of justice as conceived in most modern societies. But he is right about what needs to be achieved.

6. For example Hesiod, *Theogony* 85–87: "The people look to him [the king-judge] as he works out what is right / by giving resolutions that are fair: he speaks out faultlessly / and he soon puts an end to a quarrel however large, using his skill" (Gagarin and Woodruff [1995], pp. 19–20). Much later, Plato built his account of justice in his *Republic* to do exactly these three things, at least in an ideal city, where kinds of people would be assigned the work that is due to them, decisions about justice would be delegated to the wise, and the entire city would be harmonious in its acceptance of this arrangement, owing to the educational system.

7. See Woodruff 2005, chap. 4, "Harmony," for the range of metaphors used in ancient Greece for this concept (pp. 81–107). The weaving of disparate

elements was the best of these; the worst was Plato's idea that, in effect, all elements should sing the same tune.

8. "There is no market on Queens"—from a discussion of the relative salaries of police, MPs, and the queen, John Lucas (1980), p. 221.

9. For example, consider the case of primarily teaching versus primarily research faculty in a university. Rewarding research more than teaching may well raise the salaries of all concerned, but even so we might conclude that such a distribution represents warped values. Or perhaps not. The point is that the value issue is independent of the fairness of the distribution.

10. Recent years have seen a number of critical discussions of Rawls, many of them from philosophers who approach his work with near reverence: Lucas (1980), pp. 185 ff., strikes at a number of weaknesses in the theory. Sandel puts his finger on a point that would annoy Ajax: "If Rawls is right . . . distributive justice is not a matter of rewarding moral desert" (2009), p. 160. Cohen raises significant concerns about the use of inequality to provide incentives for good work (2008), chap. 1. Wiggins's "Neo-Aristotelian Reflections on Justice" (2006), pp. 272 ff. represent a decidedly non-Rawlsian approach. Gert objects that Rawls is committed to a view that entails the arrogance of supposing that "there is a unique right answer to every moral question" (2005), p. 384, n. 8. The most authoritative (and most respectful) criticisms come from Nussbaum (2006), esp. pp. 164 ff., and Sen (2009), pp. 52 ff. When people's capabilities are considered, wealth is a poor measure of well-being. Raz (1990) argues that Rawls's "epistemic abstinence" leaves him with too weak a theory to stand up to diversity and shows that, in any case, agreement on principles has only a modest stabilizing effect on a society.

11. Success does not by itself prove that justice rules; nor would failure show that justice has not been done.

12. *Iliad*, Book 9, lines 312–313. Achilles trusted neither the sender of the message, Agamemnon, nor its deliverer, Odysseus: "I hate like the gates of hell a man who says one thing and keeps another in his heart."

13. I thank Ruth Marcus, Elise Springer, and the discussion at Wesleyan on October 14, 2009.
14. See the excellent arguments against principle in J. S. Mill's *Utilitarianism*, chap. 5. On ethics without principles, see above p. 82, n. 1.
15. As proposed by Aristotle, *Nicomachean Ethics* 5.3.
16. On the complexity of justice in compensation, see Sheppard *et al.* (1992), esp. pp. 126–127, and Rousseau (1995), p. 219.

| Anger: Justice in the Soul

The next instant, quick as the flame from a discharged cannon at night—his right arm shot out and Claggart dropped to the deck.

—HERMAN MELVILLE, *Billy Budd, Sailor*

Imagine an Ajax who cannot feel anger. He would have accepted the insult with a smile when the prize went to Odysseus. But who would want an army of soldiers who are immune to anger?

Anger must have its due. Anger is to injustice as pain is to injury. If you do not notice pain, you may perish through unnoticed injuries. If you are unable to suffer anger, you may not recognize injustice, and so be wiped out by the transgressions of others. Billy Budd, for all his angelic goodness, has a well-developed capacity for anger. That is a good thing.[1]

Confucians try to cultivate a calmness that is immune to anger, holding it to be an emotion that clouds the mind;[2] Buddhists avoid anger in the belief that it binds us to the things of this world, thereby trapping us in the cycle of birth and death and rebirth. In the European tradition, Stoics held that anger expresses a rebellion against the Reason that guides the world, and so they too tried to learn to live without anger. But the God of Abraham can be angry, and so can Jesus; Jews and Christians are not Stoics about anger.

And they are right. A world containing Claggart is a world in which we need anger. Our capacity for anger functions as our sensitivity to injustice. Anger and justice are yoked. An individual is just insofar as his or her anger is keyed to injustice. If you tend to be too angry, or not angry enough, your sense of justice is out of whack. Even if you experience a healthy level of anger, but feel it at the wrong times, you are not properly in tune with justice. Ajax was not angry when they first took advantage of him; now he suffers delayed anger. Delaying his anger was unjust also: unjust to Agamemnon who deserved to know the truth about how he was hurting Ajax, and unjust to the whole army because Ajax was saving his anger until it was large enough to explode and threaten to destroy them as a team.

From early childhood, we are able to be angry over what we perceive to be injustice—an ability we share with other primates. As we grow up, of course, we learn how to do this better—to be less angry over the breakage of a borrowed toy, perhaps, or more angry over a subtle racial slight. Learning to be angry better is part of acquiring justice. If fairness always entailed justice, then we would expect that we could curtail anger by pointing to the fairness of a decision. But we find that this is not so, even for sophisticated adults. Fairness, as we saw earlier, is no preventer of anger.

Maybe we could solve the problem not by fixing procedures but by fixing Ajax. Most readers would like a different Ajax for this story—one who would not be liable to explode. The Ajax we want would have justice in his soul. That is Plato's way of putting it. Plato held that justice in a community depends on justice in the individuals who make up that community. Justice occurs in an individual when elements in the soul are receiving their due. Elements of the soul include the kinds of things that actually move the soul. Anger, and shame, and desire are prominent among these.

If we human beings were purely rational—if we did not have to worry about an unexpected spasm of anger or a surge of desire, then fairness would be enough for us. We would not care a hoot about honor. But we are only partly rational at best. We do care about honor, and when we care about honor, we make ourselves movable by anger. Anger may or may not be answerable to reason. Or, to put it the other way around, your reason may or may not be able to soothe your anger. Still, anger must have its due; we should not want to wipe it out, but to bring anger into harmony with reason.

The love of honor is central to human life. That is a large part of the love that moves the soldier to stay by his wounded comrade, the athlete to give her best on the field, the worker to do his fair share of the task. The gang member who kills to defend the honor of his gang is irrational. But his irrationality is not the root of our problem with him. Our problem is that his honor has become linked to a community that is at odds with the larger community in which he must live. We would be smoking a pipe dream if we thought we could make him rational and so wean him from honor. But we could hope to wean him from his smaller community, so that his love of honor would move him in more reasonable ways.

Imagine that Ajax is rational—that his reasoning power is tuned to accept whatever conclusion comes from the most reasonable argument at the time. And suppose Ajax is persuaded that the most reasonable outcome is for the armor to go to Odysseus. But suppose that this persuasion goes no deeper than his intellect. His spirit remains in rebellion. He is furious, but he tries to bear down on his fury, to control it, so that he can live with the outcome that his reason has accepted. This rational Ajax may continue as a good soldier for a time. But for that time he will be containing an explosion, and at some point he may not be able to hold it in. Justice is not good enough if it is merely mind-deep. Justice has to permeate the whole soul, into the depths where anger lives, and into the dark recesses where desires are fermenting.

Justice in the Soul

Justice in the soul helps an individual adapt smoothly to a just community. Justice cannot survive in a community unless justice has a foothold in the souls of its citizens. Plato made an excellent start on a theory of psychological justice in the *Republic*: justice is an arrangement of the human soul that prevents self-destructive internal conflict and at the same time prevents the sort of civil conflict that could destroy a community. A person whose soul is in balance, and therefore not moved by excessive desires or ambition, will not be moved to undermine the basis of a just community.[3]

Plato finds that psychological justice is analogous to justice in the community, which he holds is a harmonious arrangement of the groups that make contributions to the community. In a Platonically just community, all groups willingly make whatever adjustments to their interests are necessary for the good of the whole. That entails that each group understands the value of the contributions of the others: an Ajax would appreciate what an Odysseus does and vice versa.[4]

How are we to understand justice as a virtue? We have two alternatives:

(a) The modern approach would be to define justice first in terms of just outcomes or principles, and then define the character trait or virtue of justice as derivative: justice in character would then be the disposition to accept just outcomes or just principles.[5]

The modern approach is derived from a principled conception of justice that people will accept only insofar as they are rational. Suppose that is right. And suppose that principled justice has been established in the army, and that Ajax will not accept the outcome determined according to those principles. Then we can say that the problem is Ajax. Fix his character, and we have fixed the army. That is a standard view of Sophocles' play: Ajax is to blame. This used to be my view.

I now see, however, that we cannot understand Ajax's situation without appreciating how many Ajaxes there are, and how in some respects we are all Ajaxes. We all care about being respected; we are all subject to humiliation and anger. The most sophisticated philosopher can go berserk on finding that a colleague has been given a larger raise. But the modern approach entails rejecting Ajax and all his children as unfit to live in a community—or else reprogramming them to be more rational. But if a PhD in philosophy does not make you rational, there is not much hope for the rest of us.

We need an account of justice that allows us to give Ajax and the irrational their due.

(b) The ancient approach (the approach current before Aristotle) would be to ask what qualities both individuals and communities must cultivate in order to prevent or weather the conflicts that typically arise in communities. I will attempt to breathe new life into the ancient approach.

Plato's theory is our prime example of the ancient approach. It is built around a pragmatic goal: the cohesion of a community that allows for human irrationality to work alongside reason for the common good. Such an approach is not complete without a conception of the good for human beings—what the ancient Greeks would call *eudaimonia*, or "flourishing." The goal of justice would be the flourishing of the community through the flourishing of each of its members. An individual flourishes when his or her capacities are well developed and put to good use.[6]

For understanding justice, Plato divides the mind three ways. Part of the mind is moved by desires or appetites, part by the love of honor, and part by a yearning to know the truth. The part that yearns for knowledge is the intelligence. The part that loves honor is also the part that feels anger when honor is thwarted. Plato calls that the *thumoeides*, or spirited part. The part that is moved by desire wishes, among other things, for what riches can bring, and this part may be where greed is felt.

But greed also has a great deal to do with honor. The successful financier who insists on a huge bonus has left no desire unfulfilled—none, at least, that money could satisfy. He already has the town house, the private school tuitions, the country houses, the private jet, and the yacht. But he still insists that the world owes him a bonus.

Riches are often like the armor of Achilles, which cannot be worn by either Ajax or Odysseus. It is too small for the one and too large for the other. Rewards, even monetary ones, express a kind of honor. You and I both have all we want in the way of earthly possessions and pleasures, but I have more money than you do, and that matters to me, as a point of honor. If you get more than I, and appear to me to deserve it less, I will be angry. The distribution of rewards is mainly about honor and therefore concerns mainly the state of the honor/anger element in the human soul.

You cannot yearn too much to know the truth, but you can care too much about honor, or sacrifice too much for the satisfaction of desire. In order to be leaders, the people in charge, especially, must moderate their love of honor and their greed, or they will become, and become perceived to be, tyrants. Tyrants destroy community. Agamemnon's greed and love of honor are out of proportion, as we saw when he tangled with Achilles over their trophy women. He is enslaved to his love of honor, and that is a terrible thing in a commander.

By contrast, Ajax's defect is relatively minor: he seems immune to greed. He cares about the common goal of the army. But he comes too late and too slowly to anger, and when he comes to it he goes overboard.

Luckily for the army, Odysseus's soul is in good order. His emotions and desires at this stage are in harmony with his capacity to grasp the truth. His intelligence helps him understand Ajax's situation, to feel compassion for Ajax, and to persuade Agamemnon to let his verdict be guided by compassion. What saved the army was not the right outcome, not the right principle or procedure, not the rule of reason. What saved the army in this story was Odysseus's personal virtue, which has rubbed off on the army.

Notes

1. See Griswold (2007), pp. 43–47, "Resentment and Self-Respect."
2. For a carefully nuanced discussion of the Confucian preference for serenity, see Angle (2009), pp. 106–111.
3. See my paper "Justice as a Virtue of the Soul," forthcoming in the festschrift for Julia Annas.
4. This account of Plato is oversimple. See the account of the virtues in Plato *Republic* Book 4 and consult Annas (1999), p. 92. But note that the *Laws*, like *Republic*, shows how failures of ethical virtue lead to trouble in a city (4.716ab, where a massive failure of *sophrosune* is said to lead to chaos and is punished by divine justice).
5. See for example Williams (1980).
6. Ruth Marcus pointed this out to me: the goal of justice could not be mere survival, as that would be too low a bar. It must be *eudaimonia*.

| Honor and Respect

A concern for being equal to others tends to alienate people from themselves.

—HARRY FRANKFURT

Beatrice: "What do you want from me? They're moved out; what do you want now?
Eddie: I want my respect.

ARTHUR MILLER, *A View from the Bridge*

Respect is due to everyone who belongs in a community. Losing respect can be humiliating to an individual. A community damages its own fabric if it excludes people by denying them respect.[1] For all that, respect cannot be handed out equally to everyone; treating everyone the same blocks our ability to respect people as individuals. Respect for a person is appreciation of that person's value, accompanied by appropriate feelings, and expressed in appropriate behavior.[2]

If I respect you simply for being a human being, I am giving you what I call "generic respect," which has been considered the foundation for human rights.[3] The respect that holds a community together, however, is an appreciation of the particular value of each individual. Before a group can function at all, it has to enjoy some level of mutual respect; in a class, students and teacher must at least listen to each other with respect. Such respect has to be given before anyone has had a chance to prove his or her value to the group. So respect is an appreciation of the value that each member is presumed to have.[4]

In the circle of my small class, I offer respect to everyone in the circle, in the hope that they will return that respect to me. We show respect for each other by paying attention, not interrupting, observing the ritual of raising hands, and so on. Sometimes, a lone student rejects the respect that I offer her and insists on bullying the class and me. She has removed herself from the circle. In that case, other students make her feel the exclusion, or I speak to her about it, and she usually returns to the fold. But in a rare case she must be excluded; I may ask her to leave or join another class.

Because I offer respect to everyone in the circle, you may think that respect requires that I treat everyone the same way. But that is not the case. Students make different contributions to the class, and make their contributions in different ways. They know and feel different things. In an ideal class, the quick students listen to the slower ones with respect and find that they have something to learn from them.

Suppose a student is so painfully shy that he cannot enter discussion without suffering agonies of self-consciousness. But he is there every day, paying attention, and he contributes to the group with his writing, which, these days, shows up online. He and I talk about this. In order to respect him, I must acknowledge the particular way in which he serves as part of our circle.

What value is it that we should appreciate, by presuming it in untutored students? At a minimum it is their ability to learn, their curiosity, their preference for truth over falsehood. But above all it is their future. Confucius is reported to have said, "We should look upon the younger generation with awe because how are we to know that those who come after us will not prove our equals?"[5]

In general, a group develops mutual respect around a common commitment of some sort. In the best cases, that commitment is a form of reverence because it centers on the transcendent—on the search for truth or justice, or in service to God or the preservation of nature.

Respect is expressed in rituals of inclusion.[6] In my class, all of us in the circle are in awe of the truth about the matters we study— that is, we try to put our quest for truth above other interests we may have. Members of the circle generally do not score points at each other's expense. I do not use the occasion to reinforce my sense of superiority or my reputation for wisdom. We encourage each other to voice our disagreements—and not keep them self-ishly hoarded in our minds. But we support our views with evidence. In all of this, we observe rituals of politeness in dealing with each other. And in these ways we express reverence for truth.

Honor versus Respect

Honor is not for everyone. A few students earn grades of A. And perhaps one of them does work so splendid that I must call special attention to it, and then all of us bask in the reflected glory of this extraordinary student. We are pleased that she is one of us. The respect that holds our circle together makes it possible for us to honor this student for her brilliant work, without jealousy. We may honor different students for different kinds of achievement. But although we all respect each other, we cannot all honor each other. What goes to everyone is not an honor.

Where you give honor, you are giving respect, but not the other way around. When you give respect you are recognizing inclusion in the community; when you give honor you are recognizing unique achievements. The opposite of respect is exclusion. The opposite of honor is insult (dishonor). Insult entails exclusion, but not the other way around. Some exclusions, however, are insulting. If we withhold respect from anyone who truly belongs in our circle, that is an insult. But if we fail to give an honor, that is neither insult nor lack of respect. To be honored is a delight; not to be honored is a disappointment.

Honor and respect are essential parts of what is due in a community. When you have finished handing out salaries, divided the booty, and completed all routine promotions, you have only begun the task of justice—of giving everyone their due. Salaries are easy, respect is hard, and honors are even harder. Yet they matter enormously. Salary differences, when they matter a lot, often matter because they carry honor.

When the decision went against Ajax, he took this as an insult. A wiser man would have registered merely disappointment, if this were merely an isolated occurrence. But in the case of Ajax, this particular loss illuminates a pattern that he rightly interprets as insulting to him: the command team takes his hard work and loyalty for granted. They see him as a dumb ox who can be controlled by a simple goad, and who does not need to be recognized through any system of rewards. Understanding this, Ajax now sees that he has been insulted over time.

Belonging

How easily does the following sentence come to your tongue: "I firmly support a certain training regimen for recruits, but we have decided to give that up"? Or would you say this: "I support the regimen, but *they* have decided to give that up"? The difference between "we" and "they" is substantial; it reveals the extent to which you feel that you are a member of your department. Before the contest, Ajax would always have said "we." Odysseus, I suspect, would always have said "they," and this reflects the difference in loyalty between the two. It also explains why Ajax is far angrier than Odysseus would be if he had lost the contest. Odysseus was drafted in the army; he wants his share of the booty, but most of all he wants to go home. But for Ajax, the army is his home.

Felt membership is at the foundation of justice, and yet feelings of this sort would seem to defy any rational account of what justice requires. From the perspective of the commanders, Ajax is irrational. But their perspective is misleading; Ajax is no more irrational than they would be in similar circumstances. Ajax's behavior is in the normal human range. He should not be excluded because of his love of honor.

This could happen to you, if you are a professor reading these pages. You should be able to imagine yourself wanting to stalk out of a meeting in a black rage on learning that a clever colleague has parlayed job offers from other schools into a salary substantially more than yours—even though you have received every advancement to which faculty such as you are entitled. You are senior enough now, and well enough paid, that you do not really need a larger salary. That is why you have not been seeking outside offers. Besides, your reputation in the field is now secure, so you have slowed the pace of your research and publication. Yet you are speechless with anger to learn that this cunning dog has been honored more highly than you.

Anger at perceived inequality is widespread and not mitigated by arguments that appeal to the fairness of procedures, as we have seen. The underlying cause, I suspect, is that in an unhealthy community (such as many academic departments) we make a common mistake: we confuse honor with respect, and so we feel that because we have been denied an honor we have been denied respect. That is wrong.

A healthy community expresses respect frequently and loudly enough that its members know they are valued by their colleagues, and so are able to rejoice in honors that their colleagues receive. Perhaps they feel a twinge of jealousy; that is only human. But at least they should not feel insulted by honors given to another.

Each community must develop its own way of expressing respect. For an academic department the members might develop a habit of reading each other's work or listening to each other present research. In a staff or business situation, the solution might be meetings in which workers explain their jobs, their problems, and the solutions they have invented.

We can now state the Ajax dilemma this way: How can we prevent differences in rewards—which are inevitable in any community—from undermining a sense of mutual respect? Rules and principles alone will not help us with this dilemma. Leadership will. But leadership is hard to teach. That is because leadership calls for wisdom, and no one knows how to teach wisdom.

Notes

1. "A society is decent if its institutions do not act in ways that give the people under their authority sound reasons to consider themselves humiliated " (Margalit [1996], p. 1.).
2. See also Woodruff forthcoming, "Respect," in the *International Encyclopedia of Ethics*.
3. Darwall (1977), p. 46; Baruch Brody (1982).
4. A presumptive approach to respect is necessary in an adequate theory of generic respect as well. See Hill (2000), pp. 59–118.
5. From *Analects* 9.23; Slingerland (2003), p. 94.
6. See the section on respect in Woodruff (2001), pp. 197–203.

Wisdom

What is wise? What is the finest gift
That gods can give to mortals?

    ***

Wisdom? It's not wise
To lift our thoughts too high.
We are human, and our time is short.

—EURIPIDES, *Bacchae*, 878–79, 395–97

"Know yourself."

—*Inscription from the shrine to Apollo at Delphi*

*I*magine this: all our characters are wise.
    Agamemnon is able to appreciate Ajax's loyalty and Odysseus's cleverness at the same time, and, what is more, he can share this appreciation with the army. Even Ajax sees the value of Odysseus. Ajax is sorry that the prize did not come to him, but he understands why it went to Odysseus. After the announcement, he joins Odysseus for a party in his tent to celebrate. He is happy to see his friend rewarded.

    Of course, that is impossible for the people in our myth. But we can hope, at least, that the characters in our own stories are better than those. We should want them to be better in the direction of wisdom. Think of wisdom not as a goal you could actually reach but as a beacon marking a direction for progress.

Wisdom as Love

Wise leaders are able to appreciate the variety of the human landscape, and they bring their followers along into that appreciation. Landscapes may be easy or hard to appreciate. Anyone can appreciate a tree flaming into autumn color, or an ice-clad mountain gleaming rose-pink in a winter sunset. But the beauty of a summer bog, buzzing with living things, is not for everyone.

The human landscape is like that. The beauty of a movie star is plain for all to see, but that is rare. Luckily, we have more to see than that, and more to love. We can find beauty in the young and the old, in the fat and the thin, the athletic and the lame. Sometimes we are told of children so ugly that only their mothers could love them. But we would do better to say that only a wise observer could see their beauty. A Platonist would say that ideal beauty does not occur at all in our world, but that beauty shows up all around us in various forms, and only the wise can see it for what it is. A Christian thinker might say that evidence of God's influence is all around us, but that not everyone can see it for what it means. That is why early Christian philosophy found a friendly structure in Platonism.

Leaders see the beauty in the people who follow them. This is especially clear in the case of teachers. Think of the straight-A student who loves to learn in precisely the way the teacher loves to teach. And then, think of the student who seems to show no curiosity at all, whose mind seems to shut down totally in the classroom. Anyone can help the top students learn; such students will take any opportunity to learn, and often the teacher needs only to stand by and watch. But the students who seem to have shut down—it takes wisdom to recognize that they too have the curiosity that is our common human endowment. Their curiosity may be hidden because it is not tuned to the teacher's subject, or the teacher's methods.

Teachers need to know how to look for the beauty that is in the minds of all students. They need to bring it to light, so that other students can see it also, so that all of the class can be included in the circle of respect, so that no one will feel excluded, no one is ridiculed. Of course there should be prizes. One student is better than the others, and this should be recognized. But no one should be insulted or humiliated. And the prizewinner should learn, from the teacher's example, how to appreciate the value of the others.

The application to leadership outside the classroom is clear. To lead a team in a successful effort, you need to appreciate the different contributions the team members make, and you need to help them appreciate each other. You will need to find ways to recognize exceptional work without insulting those who are merely good.

This wisdom is a kind of love, the capacity to see beauty in unlikely places and respond to it. Love of this kind is contagious. Like justice, this wisdom is an ideal. We will never find it perfectly in any classroom or any other leadership situation. But when we do find it, we need to prize it above all other qualities in a leader. I have had teachers like this, and I now have colleagues who teach like this. I try to work this way, and I sometimes succeed. Nothing is more thrilling for a teacher.

But we all fail from time to time. Teachers encounter students they cannot teach; employers find themselves saddled with workers they cannot influence. Some students need to be expelled or transferred; some employees need to be fired or moved to jobs they may do better. Throwing someone off a team, out of a class, or out of the workplace is painful for the leader and the team. But leadership should be able to bring a team through such an experience without loss of morale; indeed, morale will improve if the team recognizes that freeloaders will be dropped.

Human Wisdom

Above all, wisdom is knowing who you are. You are a human being: you will die someday, and before then you have time to make mistakes, some of them serious. Human beings are vulnerable to error. The human situation is messy. People will not always respond to your actions as you would wish. The good decisions you make could lead to trouble, your reforms could set things back, your good deeds could be counted against you. That's what it is to be a human in a human context.[1]

You are also an individual. Let's say you are Agamemnon: you have left your wife at home while you wage the long war; you have had to sacrifice your daughter Iphigenia in order to get started on the war. Your job as leader has exacted a high price from your family, a price that has not yet been fully counted. You will find comfort at Troy with a captured princess, Cassandra, while your wife finds comfort at home with a man who will want you dead.

A cycle of killing and revenge awaits you and your family. But you would find that hard to believe now. If a prophet warns you that you will die at your wife's hand on the day of your homecoming, you will ignore him. After all, you are a commanding general, and you are about to preside over the most famous victory in history as you know it. How could things go wrong for you?

Human wisdom is not merely knowing facts. I should have said that human wisdom is *understanding* who you are, not merely knowing it. You do not have human wisdom unless you live as if you had it. Living with human wisdom involves attitudes and emotions, and these affect your actions. Living with human wisdom opens you up to the advice of others, forces you to look critically at yourself, and prepares you for things to go wrong. If you are humanly wise, you know that, despite your best efforts, you may fail, and the failure may well be your fault.

Living with human wisdom makes you a better leader, because it brings home to you the necessity of good judgment. It also makes you a better friend. Odysseus feels compassion for Ajax, even though Ajax has tried to kill him. Odysseus is able to feel compassion because his human wisdom enables him to realize that a situation as bad as Ajax's could be his own.

Wisdom as Good Judgment

Good judgment is what carries you through when you have to make a decision, and neither the facts nor the rules will make it for you. Suppose you must decide whether to order an attack while the enemy seems disorganized now or wait till tomorrow when you will have more troops but the enemy will be better fortified. Because you are only human, you cannot see into the future, and you cannot be sure that your decision on this battlefield will turn out to be the right one.

Or suppose you must decide whether to promote Ajax or Odysseus into the one higher slot that has just opened up. Because your team is locked in a complex human situation, you can't find a rule that clearly decides the matter one way or another. You don't have the safety of following a rule, and you cannot be sure how close your decision will come to being just.

You must use the best judgment you can, as a leader, but you must remember that the best judgment can turn out to have been wrong. Leaders have often exercised good judgment when their judgments turned out later to be false. We should evaluate a judgment not on the basis of the facts as they come to be known but on the basis of the evidence available at the time the judgment was made.[2]

Leaders face dilemmas often enough. By "dilemma" I mean a problem for which we cannot pull a solution out of facts or rules and regulations. You feel good reasons pulling you both ways, as Agamemnon and the others must have felt about Ajax and Odysseus. Because this is a dilemma, you have nothing to help you but good judgment. Good judgment may not seem to be worth much, because it can so easily be wrong. Yet all you have to go on is judgment, and the better your judgment is, the better for you and those who follow you.

Good judgment comes into play after you have made every effort you can to know what there is to know about the problem.

There is nothing more you could find out that would help you to make a good decision. Yet you must decide.

Good judgment asks for advice, but advice won't solve the problem. If you ask Nestor, you will get one answer. Ask Tecmessa, and you will get another. You have to decide whom to ask, you have to decide how to weigh their advice, and at the end of the day, you must decide the issue.

"I have no choice but to fire you," says the supervisor. "You don't measure up to these standards." But leaders always recognize their freedom to make choices: if they apply standards, they are choosing to apply them. Even a leader who has been ordered to apply a certain standard has the choice to resign, or to disobey orders and face the music.

There is no recipe for good judgment. That is small comfort to you as the leader. If you did have a recipe or a formula or an algorithm for deciding in tough cases, that recipe would make decisions for you, and you would not need good judgment. Moreover, after delivering your decision on the basis of a recipe, you would have something to hide behind. Often managers decide to follow a recipe and then dishonestly pretend that the outcomes are determined not by them but by the recipe. Sometimes they even fool themselves into thinking they are bound by the rules. If you choose the recipe, and the recipe determines the answer, you would be lying if you said you had no choice. You are the one who decides.

Notes

1. This is the wisdom of the tragic poems of ancient Greece, of which Sophocles' *Ajax* is a superb example. The tragic poems remind us again and again of what it is to be human, and of the danger of having ambitions that

are superhuman. The refrain of human wisdom in this tradition is *thneta phronein*—think mortal thoughts; don't suppose you could get away with acting like a divine being. For the connection between this sort of wisdom and reverence, see Woodruff (2001).

2. The judgment, in 2003, that Iraq had, or would soon have, weapons of mass destruction may well have been the best judgment that could have been made at the time, even though the world found later that it was false.

| Leadership

Before I shipped that young fellow, my forecastle was a rat-pit of quarrels. It was black times, I tell you, aboard the '*Rights*' here. I was worried to that degree my pipe had no comfort for me. But Billy came; and it was like a Catholic priest striking peace in an Irish shindy. Not that he preached to them or said anything in particular; but a virtue went out of him, sugaring the sour ones.

—HERMAN MELVILLE, *Billy Budd, Sailor*

So says the captain of the merchant ship *Rights-of-Man* to the officer who has chosen Billy Budd to be forced into the service of the *Bellipotent*, a British man-of-war. Billy is a natural leader, so good a human being that we cannot expect to meet his like. His rank is low, so that his influence does not depend on any authority he might have been given, but on his character.[1] Billy would be sickening in the work of a lesser writer than Melville. As he is, however, he is as astonishing as the sudden flowering of a spring meadow—and as hard to describe. Leaders are harder to describe than their opposites. An ideal leader is boring in literature unless he is surrounded by fascinating evil, such as that represented by Claggart in Chapter 8 of the same work:

His [Claggart's] place put various converging wires of underground influence under the chief's control, capable when astutely worked through his understrappers of operating to the mysterious discomfort, if nothing worse, of any of the sea-commonalty [the rank-and-file sailors].

Claggart is the master-at-arms, the ship's disciplinarian. He has been given the authority to have a man flogged or hanged from the yardarm. But he likes to disguise his authority. He keeps men in line through spying, bullying, lying, and veiled threats delivered by his lackeys. He is the opposite of a leader—a frighteningly bad man with authority, a tyrant.

Between them, the two characters personify Platonic ideals of good and evil. Trying to be like Billy is a lost cause, and a forbidding one at that. But trying *not* to be like Claggart is easy and inviting.

Tyrants like Claggart cannot do anything without authority granted by others; that is why they care so much to keep others in line, kicking those below them and kissing up to those above. Leaders, by contrast, can exert influence just by being who they are. A tyrant is selfish, cowardly, bullying, and arrogant. Tyrants are devoted to fear—they rule out of fear of being replaced, and they rule by striking fear into others.

Leadership is the form of power that is compatible with freedom.[2] Tyranny destroys freedom, and all forms of authority compromise freedom to some extent. You might conclude that we would be most free if we were beyond the reach of every kind of power, but that would be a mistake. Without leadership, we would not be free to do the many of the things we most want to do, which require some degree of social organization. Leadership makes freedom possible—because leadership uses its influence to help us accomplish what *we* want, as opposed to what those in authority would like us to want.[3]

When Sophocles told the story of Ajax, the memory of rule by tyrants was still fresh in the minds of his audience. Tyrants had held sway in Athens until only about fifteen years before his birth. Through most of his career, powerful forces threatened the freedom of ordinary Athenians, and a kind of tyranny would resume soon after Sophocles' death. As the Athenians began their glorious experiment with democracy, Sophocles led his fellow citizens in thinking through the difference between a tyrant and what they wanted—a leader they would want to follow enthusiastically, who would not threaten their freedom.

Tragic poems of the period, including those by Sophocles, frequently illustrate a tyrannical figure going off the rails. Such a figure shows one character trait after another that his audience did not want in a leader. Through these plays, Sophocles is giving voice to the beliefs of his audience. They are thinking thoughts like these: "Do you want to know what we want in a leader? Give us the opposite of what you see in this play. Give us the opposite of Agamemnon. Give us the opposite of any king who seems to be out for his own profit, or the profit of his cronies. Don't give us a commander who refuses to take advice, or one who prefers fixed rules to good judgment. Give us a leader."

A Leader Cultivates Qualities of Character That Others Want to Follow

These are qualities that tyrants generally do not have: honesty, courage, wisdom, reverence, compassion, good judgment, and justice. What is more, leaders provide an environment that is friendly to the development of these qualities among their followers. A tyrant tries to make people cowardly—so that they serve him out of fear; but a leader tries to make them brave.

No one actually has any of these good qualities all the time. That is why I say a leader *cultivates* good qualities of character. Honesty compels me to say of my own career as a leader that I have many times failed to rise to the level of my own ideals. For example, I believe that, as a leader, I should be attentive to what students or staff members say or think. But I have not always arranged matters so that I could listen well. Authority—along with the responsibility for making decisions—has a way of making people deaf. Leadership is hard.

Agamemnon seems to care more about his prerogatives and authority than he does about the success of his army. People sense that. For that reason they often do not trust him. When the armor goes to Odysseus, Agamemnon has such a poor reputation that it is natural for Ajax to suspect him of making a private deal with Odysseus for his own advantage.

Leaders Aim at Common Goals

Unlike a selfish tyrant, a leader aims to do what is best for all in the group or the institution. Followers, ideally, should believe that their leader has their interests at heart. Sometimes the best thing one can do for the common goal is to step down as leader. Then the leader steps down, knowing there are ways of contributing to the common goal as a follower.

Ajax has always been devoted to the army; he always put its interests ahead of his own. He has taken the army for his family. His example shows that one can care too much for the common good. He does not give his own interests sufficient weight. One can aim at common goals without sacrificing oneself.

Leaders Never Say, "I Have No Choice"

Nestor tries to give Agamemnon a set of procedures behind which he can take cover. That is good enough for some styles of management, but it undermines leadership. Leaders recognize their responsibility at every stage.

Leaders know there is no honest way to escape making choices, even if they are hedged in with rules they are supposed to follow. Still, they must decide. They do not hide behind procedures or traditions or the judgments of other people. They do not even hide behind rules.[4] The necessity of choice is frightening, and many of us seek out ways to escape it. Those ways are inherently dishonest. When leaders make mistakes (as happens often enough), they are honest about them, so as not to set bad examples—and to let others learn how to avoid similar mistakes. It takes courage to be honest; it takes courage to be a leader.

Agamemnon is afraid of rebellion. That is why he is so severe in his reaction to Ajax's madness. For another tragic example, think of Oedipus. In the famous play about Oedipus, he lashes out at people who try to help him, accusing them of trying to take his job away. He almost has his brother-in-law (who is his uncle) executed. He is prevented from doing so only by his wife (who, unbeknownst to him, is also his mother).

Oedipus is called a tyrant for several reasons, but especially because he is terrified of losing his authority as ruler. That is why Sophocles' play was named *Oedipus Tyrannus* in Greek. Not *Oedipus Rex*—that would name a legitimate ruler. A legitimate ruler has a right to authority and is not so easily frightened as one who has won power outside the law, but he still could be deposed. A true leader, however, has power through his character; no one gave that power to the leader, and no one can take it away.

Leaders Are Not Afraid of Losing Their Authority

That is partly because they don't let themselves be ruled by fear. But it is also because they are confident they can do good jobs as followers. And because they don't let their ambitions stand in the way of the goals they share with their followers. But there's more to it even than that: a leader can still be a leader without authority.

Tecmessa has no authority. She is a woman in a man's world, an army. Worse for her, she is a captured woman, a spear-bride with no rights in the family of her husband. Yet she has the strength to use the tools she has—she is brilliant, caring, and has a gift for words. She has the courage to stand up to the generals. When Ajax's soldiers are uncertain what to do, she takes charge. She fails to change the situation, but she sets a fabulous example in attempting to do so— literally fabulous; she is the stuff of fable.

Students ask: "Why talk to us about leadership? Few of us will ever get to be CEOs. None of us wants to be a general. We will be working for others for most of our lives, so your sermon on leadership is a waste of time. Why not teach us how to be good followers instead?"

When they ask this, they are confusing leadership with authority, or perhaps with management. But these are different things.

Leadership is Not the Same as Management

Management depends on some level of authority; leadership does not. Management aims at results that it wants, and that it can spell out and quantify; in doing this it sets a low bar. Under great leadership a group may do better than anyone can imagine.[5]

Good managers might try to be leaders, but leaders do not have to be managers, and may be better off not trying to be managers.[6]

Higher management, following a theory taught in books, may hedge in middle managers with rules that choke off leadership behavior and cause leadership virtues to shrink.[7] Managers may find themselves in situations in which leadership virtues will not help very much, as in a major downsizing, which would strip their authority of any graces it might have. When managers can specify what employees need to do and quantify the results, they can operate as managers—assigning incentives to levels of productivity, punishing or dismissing unproductive employees, and so forth. Their success will be limited by the knowledge and imagination of management, but the results will be fair. When the goals of an organization are not quantifiable, or when its managers do not know in advance how their team can best succeed, then leadership is called for. Leaders help us do better than either they or we think we can.

Leadership is always relevant to a mission that requires teamwork, but perhaps not when a team needs to be dismantled or reconstituted, or in other ways sculpted by authority.

Leaders Do Not Fail

Well, they may fail as managers, as politicians, as investors, as military commanders, as teachers. Leaders may be poor, unknown, defeated, unpopular, even reviled. But in being these things, they do not fail *as leaders*. The greatest leader of the Chinese tradition was Confucius, who failed at almost everything he set out to do—aside from teaching.[8] Leadership, unlike military command, or politics, or business, is not about winning battles or gaining brute power or making money. Though leadership may help you along the way to material success, you have not failed at leadership if you fail in any of these ways. A moral failure, like the huge moral failure of Claggart or the lesser one of Agamemnon, will prevent you from being a leader altogether. Agamemnon is not a failed leader; he is not a leader at all. He is, however, a general, and he comes close to failing in that role—precisely because he does not know how to be a leader.

Leaders Don't Need Authority

Anyone, at any rank, who is not afraid to speak up, or who sets an example for others, shows leadership when others follow her. Even if no one does, she is a leader in her qualities and her actions if she does what a leader does.

The only true leader in Melville's *Billy Budd* is Billy himself, who has the lowest rank of any of the main characters. Melville makes it easy for him to be a leader by making him strikingly beautiful, and making his beauty an image of his goodness. His splendid anger is precisely on target for justice, and his last words express an astonishing compassion for Captain Vere, the officer who decrees his death. Right to the end, Billy does what is best for those around him. As he rises in the noose, his shipmates hear him cry: "God bless Captain Vere!" Astonishing—but we have been prepared for this true leader also to be a true follower.

Leaders Are Good Followers

Something the military has known for ages: we can train people to be good leaders by training them to be good followers. Good followers have essentially the same skills and virtues as leaders. Good followers are not machinelike in their obedience to authority. Like leaders, they are focused on the common goal and will help the leader see the way to get there. They are independent-minded.

Leaders Think For Themselves

They are not mentally hamstrung by traditions or rules. They listen to advice from many quarters, but they are not bowled over by what others have said. In other words, they use good judgment and do their best to cultivate human wisdom. They are patient, and they take time to consider their options, when they have the luxury of doing so.

In their independence, leaders recognize that their actions set examples for others to follow. So a leader has to expect her followers to think for themselves—even if that means talking back, or standing up to her. And she should encourage that. Leaders are good learners.

Agamemnon did not like to hear anything against what he wanted to do. That was because he couldn't stand the thought of not winning in any contest. He was a terrible loser. In Book 1 of the Iliad, *he was told he must give up his trophy woman to save the army from a plague. Hearing this, he threw a tantrum and took away the trophy woman of Achilles. Whereupon Achilles threw his tantrum, the rage that almost destroyed the Greek army. That is the story of Book 1 of the* Iliad. *By being a bad loser, Agamemnon taught that same behavior to Achilles. He not only put his own interests ahead of his team's mission, he set a dreadful example for his team.*

Leaders Are Good Losers

Because they are not tyrants, they do not always get their way. They listen to others, and they may be persuaded to give up a cherished plan, or even dismiss a cherished follower. When leaders lose on such an issue, they lose well. That is because, as leaders, they are not out to win anything for themselves personally, so they take such a loss in stride. Besides, leaders make judgments that make losers of some of their followers. Leaders need to have followers who know how to be good losers, and for that they need to set good examples by losing well.

Agamemnon sometimes treated his soldiers with contempt. No wonder his soldiers treated each other with contempt. Agamemnon has done nothing to help Odysseus and Ajax appreciate each other's unique contributions to the army.

Leaders Are the Glue of Community

They nourish the conditions in which members of their group respect each other. Mutual respect will help them lose gracefully to each other when the time comes for that. More important, mutual respect will help them make the most of each other. Think of a classroom in which the quickest students actually learn from the slowest ones, because they follow the teacher's example of patient listening. Or imagine an Ajax who respects Odysseus's clever way with words.

For mutual respect there is no formula. Different communities call for different expressions of respect from their members. Respect runs all through a healthy community, and when it does, leadership follows. All are leaders, each in his or her own way, and the leader of leaders is the one who sets the tone for them all.

Leader as Poet: Ajax and Odysseus Are One

Consummate leadership takes us beyond the stereotypes. A great leader would bring the army to see how great both heroes are, how wonderful are their gifts to the army, and, in the deepest analysis, how little they actually differ. The consummate leader tells a beautiful tale, and the tale is believed. Our story of Ajax and Odysseus is very old and has taken many forms. In most versions, it turns on the classic conflict between brains and brawn, with this difference—that the ancient Greek tradition assumes that anyone who survives by his wits is a trickster, cunning, dishonest, not to be trusted.

The author of the version I follow was wiser than the tradition. Sophocles the playwright always gave his main characters the power to surprise an audience, to change in front of their eyes, to reveal unsuspected depths in response to new demands.

So it was with his treatment of Ajax and Odysseus. His Odysseus does depend on his wits, and his weapon of preference is his skill with words. But for all that, he is a man of loyalty and courage. His wits give him reasons to be loyal to Ajax. Once he sees that Ajax and his family need help, he stands by them with courage. And when his presence would be painful to them, he withdraws, compassionately. Sophocles has transformed the archetype of the hero who lives by his wits into one who uses his wits to help others—and is led to do this by his wits. A less intelligent hero would not have seen his way to stand by the man who tried to kill him.

Earlier writers had no doubt as to the justice of the case: Ajax should have won the armor; Odysseus stole it from him by means of cunning wordplay. But Sophocles is wiser. He withholds any direct verdict on the justice of Ajax's case, but from the opening scene he shows how Odysseus's wits give him a greater moral power, especially the power to be compassionate. Moreover, such success as Ajax does have in salvaging his honor comes by way of words, through Ajax's use of the art of Odysseus. So if there is a hero in this version who deserves to win, it is Odysseus. He, more than Ajax, brings the most valuable gifts to the army.[9]

As for Ajax, other writers found it all too easy to make him out to be a big dumb friendly ox who cracks under the strain of injustice. Sophocles gives us a far richer character—a man who was so strong and reliable he has never yet needed to depend on his wits, who has never had to talk himself out of a tight situation. But here is an Ajax who finds in his own depths powers no one suspected. He is a deep thinker and a persuasive speaker—clever enough to lead people astray by telling them the truth.

Sophocles is the consummate model of a leader—a poet who tells a beautiful tale compellingly. Had Agamemnon had a fraction of Sophocles' gifts, this contest would not have gone wrong. His entire audience, including the two contestants, would have understood that, no matter who is awarded the armor, Ajax and Odysseus are one in essential ways. Both are brave, both loyal, both masters of words and wit. And each would have known this about the other. In this knowledge, the one who did not win could rejoice in the other's victory.

Notes

1. In this chapter I distinguish between two kinds of power: (1) authority, such as has been granted to a commander or a manager or a dean, and can be taken away or lost; (2) influence, such as a leader can exert through character. Classical Chinese uses the same character, *te*, for power and virtue, presupposing that mere authority is not power at all.

   We use the English word "power" for a spectrum including both authority and influence, and we have a range of ideas about leadership to go with that spectrum. On different senses of power, and correspondingly different concepts of leadership, see Burns (1978), pp. 18–23.

   The character that so impresses Billy's shipmates includes a capacity for justified anger, expressed in blows, as Melville tells us from the start. They do not love him, however, because of his physical strength, but because of the way he uses it.

2. Leadership in this chapter is an ethical concept. The subject has been treated differently by writers who base their work on empirical studies and are mainly concerned with management in business. Writers who work primarily in the ethics of leadership are Johnson (2001), Badaracco (2002),

Ciulla (2003), and Ciulla et al. (2005). Brown and Treviño (2006) bring a value-based approach to management. For a broad perspective, not excluding ethics, see Burns (1978), who is the patriarch of leadership studies. For studies relating more to leadership in management, see Greenberg (2002), Chapter 11, "The Quest for Leaders." Walumbwa et al. (2008) apply values to management situations. For a strength-based approach to leadership, see Rath and Conchie (2008). For the philosophical tradition, see Cawthorn (2002).

3. A simple and elegant definition of leadership is: "the process of facilitating the accomplishment of group, organizational, or societal objectives" (Wren et al. [2009], p. 4). The definition is plainly too inclusive because every functioning member of the group in some sense facilitates the group's accomplishments. Hence the importance of the word "influence" in my account.

4 See Badaracco (2002), chap. 6, "Bend the Rules," pp. 111–126.

5. I am grateful to Reuben McDaniel for emphasizing this idea to me in conversation.

6. This follows from the definition of leadership as facilitating, through influence, the accomplishment of goals held by the group. Any member of the group can do that by developing influence outside the reins of authority. For authority, one needs a position. For influence, one needs to be a certain sort of person. See the distinction between "position-power" and "personal power," (Greenberg ([2002]), pp. 282–283).

7. A middle manager may be instructed to rate all employees, reward the top 10 percent, and fire the bottom 10 percent. Such a manager should refuse or resign, in my view, because the procedure would discourage the teamwork that a leader would want to see, teamwork that could otherwise bring the weakest team members along to success.

8. See Chin (2007) on the life and thought of Confucius.

9. Note, however, the praise Odysseus gives to Ajax, line 1340. Ajax *was* the best fighter after Achilles, as everyone agrees. Fighting, however, was not winning the war.

The Answer: How to Survive the Dilemma

What advice should you give a commander in Agamemnon's position? Suppose you have been granted a round trip to the underworld, so that you may visit with Agamemnon. You should recall that Agamemnon's pride and insensitivity led him into deeper trouble at home than it had in the army. When he came home to his wife, he brought with him a trophy woman from Troy, Cassandra. At his wife's invitation, he stepped from his chariot onto a scarlet tapestry made for the gods. He entered his palace to wash off the dust from his journey, and there, in his bathroom, he was confronted by his wife and her lover, with an ax. His wife had many reasons to be angry; not least of these was the sacrifice of their daughter Iphigenia on behalf of the army, to obtain a fair wind for the voyage to Troy. And then of course there was his long absence.

Now he has had thousands of years in the underworld to look back on his life. All this time he has wondered whether he could have done anything to save the life of Ajax, whom everyone loved so much. Suppose that, after hearing you have studied philosophy, he asks what you think he should have done.

After reading this book, I hope you would say: "Your army should have had someone with the wisdom needed to sustain it as an effective team—along with the leadership qualities to communicate that wisdom and apply it to the case. The wisdom you needed is justice. You did not have that, and neither did your army. By the time that hard decision fell into your lap—the decision about Achilles' armor— the army was seething with suspicion and discontent. It was too late then to look for wisdom. You had been foolish too long. There was nothing you could have done to save Ajax so late in the day."

Suppose Agamemnon answers, "Yes, I confess to what you say. But we won the war."

Then you should say, "That was because you were lucky. In the nick of time, when the army was in danger of coming unraveled, someone showed up who did have the required wisdom— Odysseus. That was when you were about to haul Ajax's corpse out from under his weeping child and toss it in a ravine, under guard, for scavenger dogs and birds to rip apart. Odysseus had compassion in his heart and the gift of communicating it to you all. Because of his compassion, and his good words about that, the angry troops could go back to the camp with a sense in their hearts that justice had prevailed. Justice *had* prevailed, thanks to his compassion. And so the army went back to work and won the war. You were very lucky. When you most needed justice, you had a leader as a member of your team, someone who had the wisdom that is justice and knew how to bring it home to the army. That was luck."

"You think I'm lucky! You call *this* lucky?" Agamemnon would ask, showing you the gaping ax wounds on his neck and torso.

"Ah," you should say. "Don't blame that on luck. You should have thought about your marriage long before you went to war. War is desperately hard on a marriage. There is no room for fairness between those who go to war and those who are left behind. You needed love, and beyond love you needed wisdom. And to carry that love and wisdom, you needed a steady conversation. That was missing as much in your family life as in your army. You needed to listen as much as to speak."

Agamemnon would shake his head and rumble one word, "Hopeless," turn on his heel, and merge with the throng of the dead. The truly unwise have no idea what they are missing. Proud and insensitive, Agamemnon could not learn, even from the hatred in his wife's eyes, how thoroughly he had failed in wisdom.

Afterword

AJAX AND ODYSSEUS: FROM BATTLEFIELD TO BOARDROOM

C. Cale McDowell

Few of us have sought business advice from a philosopher, but Aristophanes, the comic playwright of ancient Athens, helps us to imagine what it might be like. In *The Clouds*, he introduces us to a simple farmer, Strepsiades, whose son, Pheidippides, has developed an expensive interest in racehorses. Driven deeply into debt by his son's extravagant hobby, Strepsiades decides that the boy must learn the art of sophistry in order to defraud his creditors. But Pheidippides is not about to take lessons from the pale, barefooted man next door. Strepsiades will have to visit Socrates for himself.

Upon arriving at the small house where Socrates and his disciples have secluded themselves, Strepsiades is escorted into the presence of the great philosopher. Unwashed and flea-ridden, Socrates is suspended above the ground in a basket so that he might be closer to the Cloud goddesses who are the *genii* of his school. Strepsiades calls out to the lofty figure:

STREPSIADES: Socrates! Oh Socrates!
SOCRATES: Why do you call me, ephemeral creature?
STREPSIADES: Socrates! What are you doing up there?

SOCRATES: I walk on the air in order to look down on the sun.

STREPSIADES: But why do you need to float on a rack to scorn the gods? If you have to do it, why not do it on the ground?

SOCRATES: In order that I may make exact discoveries of the highest nature! Thus, my mind is suspended to create only elevated notions. The grains of these thoughts then merge with the similar atmosphere of thin air! If I had remained earthbound and attempted to scrutinize the heights, I would have found nothing.[1]

How far removed are the thoughts of Socrates from the business concerns of earthbound Strepsiades! What could an eccentric, dangling in a basket, have to teach a man who has lived his life on solid ground? Not much, Aristophanes suggests, and in so doing, he gives us the persistent image of the philosopher, disconnected from the real world, with his head in the Clouds.

This is not entirely unfair. Even Plato's Socrates—recalling the story of Thales, who while gazing aloft at the stars fell into a well—offers support for the representation of the philosopher as comically detached and practically useless (*Theaetetus* 172c–176a). Unable to find his way to the agora, to argue convincingly before an audience of worldly men, or even to make his own bed, the philosopher, it seems, is the last person one should ask for help in navigating real-world dilemmas. Content in the abstract realm of the Forms, he focuses his thoughts on "the deeps below the earth" and "the heights above the heavens...never condescending to what lies near at hand."[2]

Though practical business concerns are not the usual purview of the philosopher, Paul Woodruff has shown us that justice and the pragmatic elements of management are inextricably linked. As a philosopher and practiced leader, Woodruff understands justice in all the messy human complexity too readily ignored by theorists focusing only on the precise and abstract, unburdened by empirical knowledge. Woodruff's particularism eschews unchanging rules in favor of a humanistic approach always contingent on "what lies near at hand." In the pursuit of business goals and transcendent justice alike, he does not miss the well for the stars.

The result is a book that is both philosophy and field manual. The lessons of *The Ajax Dilemma* promise to shed new light on some of the most intractable problems recognized by management theorists and faced daily by leaders in every field. Indeed, we have much to gain if we can apply what Woodruff has learned from the warriors at Troy to our own management dilemmas. The discussion that follows is intended to stimulate additional thought along these lines.

Fixed Rules in Business and Law

> *To rest upon a formula is a slumber that, prolonged, means death.*
> —OLIVER WENDELL HOLMES[3]

The story of Ajax and Odysseus demonstrates that rules and principles, though reasonable on their face, may fail under the stress of daily use and unanticipated circumstances to yield just outcomes. Many of the great practitioners of justice have struggled with this reality, searching first for immutable principles and only with experience becoming reconciled to some degree of uncertainty. Such was the path of Benjamin Cardozo:

> I was much troubled in spirit, in my first years upon the bench, to find how trackless was the ocean on which I had embarked. I sought for certainty. I was oppressed and disheartened when I found that the quest for it was futile. I was trying to reach land, the solid land of fixed and settled rules, the paradise of a justice that would declare itself by tokens plainer and more commanding than its pale and glimmering reflections in my own vacillating mind and conscience. I found with the voyagers in Browning's *Paracelsus* that "the real heaven was always beyond."[4]

Oliver Wendell Holmes harbored a similar affinity for certainty and abstraction, having written in 1899 that "all the pleasure of life is in general ideas."[5] But, for Justice Holmes, who would later opine in his famous *Lochner* dissent that "general propositions do not decide concrete cases,"[6] fixed universal rules were no way to arrive at real-world solutions: "All the use of life is in specific solutions—which cannot be reached through generalities any more than a picture can be painted by knowing some rules of method. They are reached by insight, tact and specific knowledge."[7]

Justice cannot be delivered on autopilot. It must be sensitive to the thickness and complexity of human experience and is achieved only by inquiry into the facts of the case at hand. The judge who knows (to borrow from Richard Posner) that "he is not Apollo's oracle...that he must take personal responsibility for his decisions rather than suppose them made in heaven of

Platonic legal forms," may have the humility to see that, at least in some cases, man-made rules must give way to facts.[8] As Judge Posner has explained, "circumstances configure the judicial role, and circumstances change."[9]

Circumstances also configure the role of the manager. But managers, like judges, are not immune to the siren song of fixed and settled rules. The sirens sing of clarity, transparency, and managerial discipline. But, as Paul Woodruff has shown us, rules cannot supplant good judgment. What we really need is leadership.

Wanted: Unprincipled Manager

Beware of geeks bearing formulas.
> —WARREN BUFFETT, *Letter to Shareholders of Berkshire Hathaway, February 27, 2009*

Suppose that we want to open a chain of gyro stands on the Trojan plane. We will want a manager who is capable of assembling a team of employees, each well suited to his particular role, keeping the team together through inevitable strains and stresses, and ultimately earning us a healthy return on our investment.

Who, then, will we put in charge of our venture? Certainly not Nestor, if his approach to management is anything like his procedural approach to justice. Recall that Nestor was ultimately unconcerned with outcomes so long as the process was fair. But, as business owners, our interests lie in results, not process. We want a manager who will monitor the operations of our business and adjust as necessary to achieve our ends. Surely, we might be tempted to think, Nestor would abandon his procedural orientation if we were to give him an interest in the profits of the company. But he has more than money at stake in the war, and there he is willing to accept bad outcomes if they result from good processes. Well intending as he may be, Nestor is no more likely to deliver business results for us than justice for Ajax and Odysseus.

Perhaps, then, Odysseus could run the business. He understands as well as anyone the importance of achieving good results. But we know that his particularism will be increasingly difficult to maintain as our business grows. With new gyro stands, we will need more midlevel managers and individual contributors, not all of whom will have Odysseus's knack for finding the right outcome. In some cases, even the best managers will be accused of acting capriciously, or worse, discriminatorily. Some will yearn for policies and procedures to guide their hands, easing the burden of unconstrained decision making.

History shows that we are likely to put Agamemnon in charge. He is an experienced king and general who knows how to run a large organization. And, yet, he is so bound by principles that he is unable to deviate from them, even when they threaten to destroy his army. What, then, do we risk when we put Agamemnon in charge of our business? Consider the following scenario:

Scenario 1: Agamemnon implements a rule-based incentive compensation plan and hires one of his soldiers, Thersites, to run his first gyro stand. Thersites is told that his bonus will be based on a formula taking into account the number of gyros sold, improvements to market share, and customer satisfaction, as measured by a survey. Thersites achieves his unit sales goal, but he does so by readily offering deep discounts, destroying Agamemnon's profit margin. He improves his market share by focusing excessively within his existing sales area rather than branching out into less saturated areas to acquire new business at lower cost. And he meets his customer satisfaction target by telling his less satisfied patrons to take a hike. For all of this, Thersites will receive a bonus, but he certainly will not have earned it.

True to form, Thersites has undermined Agamemnon at every opportunity.[10] Agamemnon may have attempted to take all possible contingencies into account in designing his incentive program, but Thersites has managed to turn his own rules against him. He has frustrated Agamemnon's ultimate goals not by breaking the rules but by following them too closely. Employees have an uncanny ability to distort outcomes in this way, especially when it suits their own interests. Indeed, there is a little Thersites in us all.

To illustrate further, let us consider a distinctly modern scenario:

Scenario 2: Nick runs a team of computer programmers for a large software company, which has asked him to develop an incentive program to improve productivity. In year one, he implements a bonus plan that rewards programmers who produce the most lines of code. The result is long, sloppy algorithms. In year two, Nick refines his approach to take quality into account. Programmers earn points for lines of code written and lose points for errors and inefficiencies. The result is a loss of appetite for innovation. Why enter uncharted waters when cutting and pasting old code, tried and true, is the surest path to a bonus? In year three, Nick attempts to reward innovation and creativity, with the result that programmers become too eager to reinvent the wheel at the cost of efficiency.

We have now seen that rule-based incentive programs can produce unanticipated, and often perverse, results. You may be tempted to think that you could design an incentive program that works in all possible circumstances. But even the most carefully designed rules can go awry in day-to-day use. Let us return to Troy for a final example:

Scenario 3: Agamemnon, Nestor, and Odysseus each run a cluster of our gyro stands. Agamemnon compensates his gyro peddlers on the basis of net profits, the outcome most important to him. Nestor's compensation scheme is based on units sold. It would unfairly shift the risk of business ownership to his employees, he thinks, if he were to reward them on the basis of net profits. After all, salesmen control only sales revenue, and not expenses. Odysseus has no rules for compensation, but he has earned the trust of his employees, who know that they will be rewarded justly for their contributions at the end of the day. As the war progresses, our managers find that beef and pork, the ingredients of the gyros, are becoming scarcer and more expensive, while the market is not likely to bear higher gyro prices. Nestor's peddlers continue as usual—they can sell as many units as before, and earn their bonuses, despite the fact that the business is on its way to failure. Agamemnon's gyro peddlers, whose compensation is based on net profits, have to find a solution if they wish to earn bonuses. They decide to supplement profits by selling wine, which does the Greeks no favors on the battlefield. Odysseus's gyro peddlers know that, unlike Nestor's salesmen, they must adapt to earn their bonuses, and, unlike Agamemnon's salesmen, they must adapt responsibly. Their solution is to use mutton, rather than the increasingly expensive beef and pork. With the clarity of hindsight, Odysseus will reward his salesmen for actively contributing to the business without hindering the larger war effort.

An effective pay-for-performance system does not set boundaries on the means by which employees may add value. It must be flexible enough to reward contributions that cannot be anticipated by a rule maker. Nestor's plan was to craft a reward system holding employees accountable only for those elements that they directly control. But by limiting the factors on which his employees were evaluated, Nestor also limited the extent to which their short-term interests were aligned with his own. By narrowing the scope of his employees' responsibility, Nestor removed their felt incentive to find creative solutions to difficult problems. In the long run, when Nestor's gyro stands go out of business, he and his employees will suffer the consequences together.

The interests of Agamemnon and his employees were better aligned with respect to the business, but apparently not with respect to the war. Who could have guessed that the employees' pursuit of profits would have resulted in an army of drunken soldiers? By measuring and rewarding on the basis of only one criterion, Agamemnon blinkered his employees to an array of other important considerations.

Rule-based incentives are no substitute for good judgment and goodwill. An incentive system relying heavily on rules and policies will, at best, fail to contemplate the full range of beneficial activities in which employees may be engaged and, at worst, undermine the ultimate goals of the organization.

Decentralization and Inherent Rewards

And they set to, a handful of men, full of confidence, and they made bricks and dug up to the earth. Never have men worked more rapidly, for they all had one thought, one aim and one dream.

—METROPOLIS[11]

The Agamemnon of this story distrusts Ajax for being "his own man." For him, the rule is simple: soldiers follow orders. Ajax sees Agamemnon as a friend, while Agamemnon sees Ajax as an implement of war, whose role is to apply his brawn in furtherance of his commander's ends. Friendship would be too complicated, too reciprocal, and too much for a mere soldier to ask. Our Agamemnon wants obedience, and nothing else, from Ajax.

A better Agamemnon would have taken a different approach. "No need," he would tell Ajax and his peers, "to give orders to such leaders of the Argives as you are, for of your own selves you spur your men on to fight with might and main."[12] One imagines that Ajax would prefer to fight under this commander in chief, and might even do a better job.

In the wars of the twenty-first century, our own military leaders have had to relearn this lesson, understood not so long ago by military commanders like Clausewitz and Moltke the Elder, who knew the limits of rules and systems in the uncertain environment of warfare.[13] Modern warfare calls for less emphasis on grand plans rife with tactical detail and for more emphasis on mission command through decentralized operations. Nimble insurgencies move too quickly for an army that runs every tactical decision up the flagpole. Today's counterinsurgency operations require soldiers at all levels who are capable of understanding the objective and prepared to accomplish their commanders' intent by acting "intelligently and independently without orders."[14] In counterinsurgency, "senior leaders set the proper direction and climate with thorough training and clear guidance; then they trust their subordinates to do the right thing."[15]

Early Management Theory

Decentralization is still relatively new to management theory. Indeed, much of the management orthodoxy of the twentieth century was based on the "scientific management" principles articulated by F. W. Taylor, who called for foremen to take control of all facets of their employees' work.

Taylor expressed his view of the average worker in his parable of Schmidt, a hardworking Pennsylvania Dutchman whose job was to handle pig iron for the Bethlehem Steel Company. Schmidt's job, we are told, is "perhaps the crudest and most elementary form of labor which is performed by man," carried out by workers who are "heavy both mentally and physically," and so simple that "it would be possible to train an intelligent gorilla so as to become a more efficient pig iron handler than any man can be."[16]

Schmidt is a purely economic being, motivated only by financial rewards and penalties. Unlike most pig iron handlers, who work inefficiently and at the pace of their slowest teammate, Schmidt is naturally a hard worker. But, like the others, he is "so stupid and so phlegmatic that he more nearly resembles in his mental make-up an ox than any other type."[17] An intelligent man, Taylor explains, would be "entirely unsuited to what would, for him, be the grinding monotony of work of this character."[18]

When Taylor studied the work of Schmidt and his gang, he found that each man, on average, was handling 12.5 long tons of pig iron per day, while Taylor had determined that a proper day's work amounted to 47 long tons.[19] By regulating Schmidt's movement and pace, and the intervals at which he rested, Taylor was able to achieve sustainable output at the desired level. Had Schmidt been left to his own devices, he would have worked too slowly, wasting valuable time, or too quickly, tiring himself out. In short, there is a "science" to Schmidt's work, but he will never understand it. Instead, he must be trained and closely supervised by "a man more intelligent than himself" so that he may work in accordance with the science of his trade.[20] He must do "just what he's told to do, and no back talk."[21]

Taylor built his system of scientific management around this dim view of workers. Under his direction, manufacturing was transformed from a process driven by skilled tradesmen into one controlled entirely by managers, who established "rules, laws, and formulae which replace the judgment of the individual workman."[22] Managers boosted output by manipulating the work environment and doling out simple wage incentives. Through motion and time study, complex trades were broken into simple, repetitive tasks, and each traditional rule of thumb or worker preference was replaced by a scientifically determined "one best way."[23]

Taylor's ideas dominated management theory until they were challenged by a series of studies conducted between 1924 and 1932 at the Hawthorne Works of the Western Electric Company in Chicago.[24] The design of the first round of experiments—intended to determine the effect of changes in lighting on the productivity of workers—was not inconsistent with the assumptions of Taylor's scientific management. In these experiments, workers were exposed to varying levels of light while performing their jobs. As expected, when the level of illumination was increased for the experimental group, output rose. Strangely, however, output also rose for the control group, which had been exposed to a constant level of illumination. As the lights were raised again for the experimental group, both the experimental and control groups continued to perform better. Even more surprisingly, as the lights were lowered to their original levels, both groups continued to improve.

Because early experiments failed to prove the expected relationships between output and the physical work environment, additional experiments were planned. Researchers would now investigate the effect on productivity of various changes to employee compensation and working conditions. Over time, it became apparent that the many variances introduced by researchers could not account for the steady rise in employee productivity. Researchers concluded that the increases in productivity were driven not by changes in the physical work environment, working schedules, or even pay but rather by the collaborative relationship between supervisors and workers and a sense on the part of the employees that they were members of a special group, working toward a common goal, and taking part in a meaningful activity. Due to these intangible changes, employees involved in the experiments became simultaneously happier, more independent, and more productive.

While the Hawthorne studies have been criticized on methodological grounds, they have succeeded in helping us to see management as a humanistic exercise, lending support to what is now called the "human relations" movement in management theory. For members of the human relations school, employees can enjoy their work, appreciate a challenge, and derive inherent rewards from advancing a shared agenda under supportive management. Workers can be self-motivated and creative, and they can often be trusted to exercise good judgment. This more optimistic view of employees has encouraged managers to treat workers as members of a team with common goals, to delegate responsibility, and to take steps to foster job satisfaction.

F. W. Taylor's attempt to rationalize the workplace had trapped the employee in Max Weber's iron cage of bureaucracy, reducing him to "a single cog in an ever-moving mechanism which pre-scribed to him an essentially fixed route of march."[25] Taylor's management system failed to motivate and reward employees because it treated them as machines with narrow functions and no discretion, depriving them of the rewards intrinsic to their work.

Given the right opportunities, Ajax has the capacity to share with Odysseus in rewards transcending his paycheck. Many orga-nizations have found that this also accretes to the bottom line, as employees are at their most productive when afforded the oppor-tunity to work with a reasonable degree of autonomy, making tac-tical decisions and exercising initiative within a broad strategic mandate. After all, employees who are empowered to make decisions are more likely to innovate, and those operating in the field often have better information than senior managers, permit-ting them to act quickly in response to changing circumstances. As the U.S. military has learned in its counterinsurgency operations, modern warfare "places a premium on leadership at every level, from sergeant to general."[26]

The same holds true in the world of commerce, where many organizations now offer their employees a chance to influence the agenda, not merely the means of implementation. "Look at why big companies die," says Shari Ballard, an executive vice president at Best Buy. "They implode on themselves. They create all these systems and processes—and then end up with a very small percentage of people who are supposed to solve complex problems, while the other 98% of people just execute. You can't come up with enough good ideas that way to keep growing."[27] Companies that depend on rapid innovation have long understood the importance of decentralization, and there are many success stories. When Google asked its engineers to use 20 percent of their time to work on their own ideas and projects, it struck a rich vein of creativity that has resulted in some of the company's most successful products.[28] Google understands that innovation is most easily cultivated where the company's mission overlaps with the passions of its individual employees, and it empowers them to work autonomously within that space. "Google works from the bottom up," says software engineer Bharat Mediratta. "If you have a great technical idea, you don't have your V.P. send out a memo telling everybody to use it. Instead, you take it to your fellow engineers and convince them that it's good."[29]

For good employees, financial rewards are necessary but rarely sufficient. Of equal importance are the intrinsic rewards associated with a job well done under self-direction and toward a compelling end. Employees work hardest and smartest when they understand what they are working toward and believe it to be worth their time.

Multisource Performance Appraisal and the Limitations of Fairness

"Et tu, Brute? Then fall, Caesar."

—JULIUS CAESAR, *according to Shakespeare*

When the Greeks of this story need a process by which to award Achilles' armor, their thoughts turn to panels and polls. Agamemnon avoids accusations of partiality by submitting the question to a panel made up of the peers of Ajax and Odysseus. What could be fairer than that? And when Odysseus argues on his own behalf, he appeals to the judgment of the Trojans. Whose opinion could matter more?

Many companies allocate rewards in much the same way, using mechanisms like the so-called 360-degree (or multisource) performance appraisal.[30] Under these systems, input is taken from the full range of individuals who work with the person under review—superiors, peers, subordinates, and often customers. Some businesses have put these systems to good use, especially for the purpose of receiving informal feedback. However, as management experts have noted, multisource performance appraisal can be dangerous when it is linked directly to rewards and penalties.

Julius Caesar received a multisource performance appraisal on the Ides of March. The first to appraise his work was Publius Servilius Casca, who stabbed him in the neck. Caesar fought his attackers until spotting among them his friend Marcus Brutus. Brutus was not out for power, money, or revenge. His motive was noble, and his actions were for the good of Rome. His presence in the company of the attackers meant that Caesar could trust none of his allies. More importantly, it meant that this was no mere power grab.

That could be no consolation to Caesar, who would surely have rather died as the victim of a wrongful coup than as a tyrant overthrown. The involvement of Brutus in some way legitimized the plot, which must have stung more than the collective malice of his many coconspirators. Caesar simply gave up when he saw Brutus, not because he accepted his assassination as just but because he knew it was not worth fighting to be part of a community that could so roundly reject him. So, resigned to his fate, he pulled his toga over his head and withdrew.

Perhaps Caesar and Ajax could not have been saved, but wayward employees often can. The best employees want to be part of the team. They are willing to fight to prove their worth and their place in the organization. Highly committed employees can be put back on course with a minor adjustment to heading, but they are prone to overcorrection. When Ajax learned what his peers thought of him, he decided that he could no longer be a part of the community to which he had been so committed just days before.

Performance appraisal systems that incorporate feedback from many sources are attempts at procedural fairness—Nestor's brand of justice. But, as we have seen, fairness does not always promote justice and, in some cases, runs against it. Caesar and Ajax were most deeply hurt by what was most indicative of fairness—in Caesar's case, the involvement of Brutus, and, in Ajax's case, the involvement of his peers.

Scenario 4: Stephen is the high-billing senior associate at a small law firm that sets compensation partly on the basis of subjective criteria. One year, Susan, the managing partner, sets Stephen's compensation below what he believes he deserves. Stephen meets with Susan to express his dissatisfaction. Susan explains her belief that Stephen's compensation has been set at an appropriate level, given his lack of attention to client development. But after listening to his complaints, she suggests, "To be completely fair, let's take this matter to a full meeting of the partners." Stephen consents, and the partners quickly side with Susan. Now Stephen is planning his exit from the firm.

In an environment of shared governance, where legitimacy and power are drawn from the same well, a showing of fairness is easily mistaken for a showing of force. The partners' quick dismissal of Stephen's complaint not only carried with it a new level of finality, placing Stephen's goal further out of reach, but also drove a wedge between him and the rest of the firm. After the meeting, Stephen was at odds not merely with his managing partner but with the firm as a whole. So, like Caesar and Ajax, he decided to throw in the towel.

Sometimes, managers promote justice by interposing themselves between an individual and the larger community. Had Susan not asked the other partners to ratify her decision, she might have communicated the point about client development to Stephen without causing him to feel hopelessly at odds with the team as a whole. In cases where a push is enough, managers should remember that often committees can only shove.

Standardization and the Management of Large Groups

> "Yes, it's true he was as strong as four ordinary men, but I'll have no trouble finding the four ordinary men to take his place."
>
> —AGAMEMNON, *in Woodruff's narrative*

"One more victory against the Romans, and we shall be utterly ruined."

—PYRRHUS OF EPIRUS, *according to Plutarch*[31]

Agamemnon will not miss Ajax, because what Ajax gave him is easily replaced. Few are less fortunate than those who go to war under a commander with this outlook, but it has happened often.

Pyrrhus led his army of Greeks from Epirus against the Romans at Heraclea in 280 BC and at Asculum in 279 BC in what has come to be called the Pyrrhic War. At Heraclea, in this first ever meeting of the Greek phalanx and the Roman legion, neither side was able to gain the upper hand until Pyrrhus employed his technological advantage—elephants. At Asculum, the Romans were prepared with anti-elephant devices, and the terrain was inhospitable to the Epirotes' cavalry. Again, the two sides fought at length before either gained a clear advantage. Finally, the Epirotes were victorious.

By all accounts, Pyrrhus lost fewer soldiers in these battles than did the Romans, but his casualties were more deeply felt. This was true for two reasons. First, he lost many of his best generals and advisers—the sons of Odysseus. Second, his soldiers were less easily replaced, and thus more valuable, than the Roman legionnaires, who were replenished with ever-increasing vigor.

Military leaders have often attempted to substitute large numbers for clever strategy, and always at great human cost. This was the case during the American Civil War, when Ulysses S. Grant, confident that the resources and manpower of the Union would outlast the Confederate army, employed a policy of attrition resulting in tremendous casualties on both sides. Grant's policy stands in stark contrast to that of the United States in Afghanistan, where our appetite for attrition is far lower than the insurgents', and the so-called insurgent math dictates that every casualty on the side of the insurgency results in many more eager conscripts.[32]

Like Rome's legionnaires and Grant's Union troops, Ajax often finds himself a member of a large, homogenous group. This is a major source of his vulnerability, often causing him to be viewed, like one of Al Qaeda's insurgents, as an expendable resource. From the perspective of the manager, it costs relatively little to lose members of a large group. In some cases, it also costs more to reward them and saves more to cut their pay:

Scenario 5: Lara, the CFO of a large state university facing deep budget cuts, has been asked by her boss to identify potential areas of savings. The university operates a system of classified employee titles, each of which has a standardized pay range. Lara finds that the university employs 10 vice presidents, 15 deans, 35 associate deans, 60 assistant deans, 200 executive assistants, and 450 administrative assistants. Her gaze fixes on the administrative assistant title, where small changes to the pay range might produce relatively large savings.

The fact that Ajax often holds a rank with standardized pay makes him still more vulnerable, as this may render individual pay increases impossible, classwide pay increases prohibitively expensive, and classwide pay cuts disproportionately attractive. Thus, in an organization with standardized pay, compensation decisions must be carried out largely at the level of a class of employees and are less likely to be favorable.

Indeed, while employers have often standardized compensation schemes in the interest of fairness, standardization is among the greatest enemies of justice in the distribution of rewards. Justice requires attention to individuals and circumstances, but standardization entails precisely the opposite. In its strongest forms, standardization causes pay to become entirely dissociated from individual performance, leaving no room for the rewards that a healthy community bestows on individuals in recognition of meritorious service. In this regard, the compensation mechanism of the United States civil service is a useful case study.

Standardization in the Civil Service

The foundation of the modern U.S. civil service system was laid in the wake of President James Garfield's assassination in 1881 by a campaign worker who believed his support of the president should have earned him a diplomatic post. In 1883, Congress passed the Pendleton Act, which marked a shift away from the political patronage of the spoils system and set the stage for the standardization of pay within the civil service. Under the Pendleton Act, prospective employees would compete openly for federal jobs on the basis of neutral examinations and, once hired, would be protected from political coercion. Congress was said to have created a neutral "merit system," but merit-based rewards and neutrality were uneasy bedfellows. To the extent that managers had the power to reward employees for their individual merit, they also had the power to introduce subjectivity and bias. To ensure full neutrality, it seemed, employee rewards would have to be standardized.

In the coming years, Congress would take a number of steps to depersonalize the civil service, implementing many of the scientific management principles espoused by F. W. Taylor. By 1923, Congress had adopted a system associating rank and pay with position rather than personal qualifications, in contrast to the rank-in-person systems still employed by the military and the Foreign Service.[33] By 1949, Congress had implemented the basic structure of the familiar General Schedule, which today divides federal jobs among a series of fifteen grades, each with a ten-step pay band. Under the General Schedule, employees exhibiting an "acceptable level of competence" move from step to step within their pay bands, earning raises keyed primarily to length of service.[34]

The classification of federal positions was intended to help the government achieve its objective of neutrality. As one commentator explained, the civil service would be "like a hammer or a saw; it would do nothing at all by itself, but it would serve any purpose, wise or unwise, good or bad, to which any user put it."[35] But employees are not hammers or saws. They do not fit neatly into categories or move at the same pace along uniform career paths. Because it is incapable of recognizing employee differences, a standardized civil service leaves no room for rewards, which shortchanges both employee and employer. The General Schedule may shield employees from political influence and managerial bias, but it is just as likely to deny the best and hardest-working employees their just compensation while propping up their mediocre colleagues. And by compensating the latter as well as the former, the General Schedule fails to encourage improvement.

Senior civil servants and politicians have long worried about the effect of the General Schedule on the government workforce, and for good reason. Indeed, it seems neutrality and standardization are inimical to the ideal of high performance. Unavoidably, the government's emphasis on neutrality puts it at a disadvantage, as a dispassionate staff of neutral bureaucrats lacks the intrinsic motivation to perform at the level of engaged partisans.[36] Likewise, the standardization of pay under the General Schedule precludes the effective deployment of financial rewards as incentives, denying managers the power to align employee interests with organizational goals. Alas, government managers are left with almost none of the tools that their private sector counterparts use to encourage employee excellence.

Thus it is no surprise that, in a recent survey of top government human resources officers, more than two-thirds of participants favored eliminating or significantly reforming the General Schedule, citing its inflexibility and its failure to link pay to performance.[37] Some participants did appreciate the General Schedule's transparency and consistency, but transparency is not an unqualified good,[38] and, as Paul Woodruff has shown us, consistency is a path to mere fairness, not justice. As one top government human resources executive explained, "The best thing [about the General Schedule] is that it's predictable; the worst thing is that it's predictable."[39] Neutrality in the civil service is a worthy goal, but when implemented by way of rule-driven standardization, it comes at too great a cost.

Forced Differentiation

When we were making a baseball team, the best players always got picked first, the fair players were put in the easy positions, usually second base or right field, and the least athletic ones had to watch from

*the sidelines. Everyone knew where he stood. The top kids wanted
desperately to stay there, and got the reward of respect and the thrill
of winning. The kids in the middle worked their tails off to get better,
and sometimes they did, bringing up the quality of play for everyone.
And the kids who couldn't make the cut usually found other pursuits,
sports and otherwise, that they enjoyed and excelled at. Not everyone
can be a great ballplayer, and not every great ballplayer can be a
great doctor, computer programmer, carpenter, musician, or poet.*

—JACK WELCH[40]

*"First prize is a Cadillac Eldorado.... Second prize is a set of steak
knives. Third prize is you're fired."*

—BLAKE, *Glengarry Glen Ross*[41]

Rewards are necessarily rooted in differentiation. The most powerful rewards are distributed equitably but never equally. They are scarce and hard-won, wanted by all but enjoyed by few. At their best, rewards recognize individual merit in a way that incentivizes good performance and strengthens community. But we have also seen the power of rewards to bruise egos, damage relationships, and destroy community. The distribution of rewards is not for the faint of heart.

At its core, *The Ajax Dilemma* is a problem of allocating scarce resources in the form of rewards. Odysseus and Ajax are the two greatest living heroes of the Greek army, and Agamemnon can reward only one of them with the armor of Achilles. Managers work within a similar framework when they hire, fire, promote, and compensate employees. The allocation of rewards is one of the most important, and most difficult, things that a manager does. In an ideal world, managers would unflinchingly hand down decisions that invariably achieve just outcomes congruent with their pragmatic ends. But these decisions are rarely easy, and there are no sure paths to the right answers.

One of the best known, and most controversial, systems for allocating rewards in the private sector comes from Jack Welch, the former CEO of General Electric. In stark contrast to the U.S. Civil Service, Welch's system forces meaningful differentiation. The system—known as the "vitality curve," or "20-70-10"—requires that managers "cultivate the strong and cull the weak" by using performance-based classifications to guide all promotion and salary decisions.[42]

At GE, Welch applied 20-70-10 to allocate resources among both business units and people. He asked managers to sort their employees into the top 20 percent, middle 70 percent, and bottom 10 percent. Members of the top 20 percent are the company's best and brightest. They receive abundant praise, high salaries, bonuses, and opportunities for advancement. The middle 70 percent is the bulk of the workforce. If carefully managed, some will rise into the top 20 percent. The bottom 10 percent is the group of low performers who must ultimately improve or be "managed out" of the organization. Welch's 20-70-10 system is by no means the only rigid employee differentiation scheme used by businesses. In 2006, for example, it was reported that Yahoo! had implemented a "stack ranking" system whereby employees in each unit were ranked from best to worst, and all raises, bonuses, and promotions were distributed accordingly.[43]

Employee differentiation systems of this type are zero-sum games. When one employee moves up into the top 20 percent, another must drop down to the middle 70 percent. Ideally, this should foster healthy competition, driving productivity and "bringing up the quality of play for everyone," as Welch puts it.[44]

Were it not for spine-stiffening employee differentiation systems, perhaps too many managers would give in to the temptation to spread rewards thinly and evenly, scattering precious resources to the winds. Such an even-handed approach may avoid hurt feelings for the short term, but likely at great cost to the organization. Employee differentiation systems are, thus, designed to force mediocre managers to make tough decisions on the basis of merit. But, in so doing, these systems risk robbing good managers of the flexibility they need to act in the best interests of their organizations while also preserving the inherently delicate communities in which they work.

In the private sector, we generally expect managers to compensate employees on the basis of individual merit, but sometimes circumstances require otherwise. Consider the managerial dilemmas posed by the free market. An employee's value in the market is, in some sense, tied to merit, but no large organization can perfectly reconcile its internal evaluations of merit with its market-driven salaries. Indeed, in a complex environment characterized by vigorous competition for human talent, managers must be able to make some resource allocation decisions without the benefit of strictly merit-based reasons. This can present serious challenges, as the resource allocations necessary for an organization's competitiveness may conflict with the perceptions of justice held by its individual members, and market-based justifications are rarely any consolation to lower-earning employees.

Scenario 6: Kate, a program manager for a high-tech manufacturing company, has been given a 2 percent merit raise pool and told that she must allocate all raises on the basis of a stack ranking employee differentiation system. She is two months away from the launch of a major new product, and her engineers are short on time. David, a mediocre engineer, has received an offer to join a competing company, which he is seriously considering. Under normal circumstances, David's departure would be an opportunity to find a better engineer to take his place, but Kate knows she will not make the product launch deadline if she has to train his replacement now. If she wants to retain David until after the product launch, she will have to give him a raise. And, given the constraints under which she must operate, that means ranking him above more qualified engineers.

Under her company's stack ranking system, Kate has been given the power to allocate resources as rewards and nothing else. If Kate ranks her engineers according strictly to merit, she will lose David to her competitor and miss the product launch deadline. If she artificially increases David's ranking to make him eligible for a raise, she may retain him and meet the deadline, but she risks undermining the morale of David's more competent peers, possibly to her department's longer-term detriment. Reasonable managers may disagree about the best approach in such a case, but Kate has a plausible reason for allocating some of her department's resources on a basis other than merit, and only she has the information necessary to make a fully informed decision.

Even without a rigid employee differentiation system, Kate would face a difficult choice. If she decides that she should retain David, she must try to do so without causing her other employees to feel that he has been unjustly rewarded. The odds are already stacked against her. A raise will tend to carry the weight of reward, and the attendant powers of honor and insult, regardless of whether it is imparted for the purpose of reward or retention.

If Kate is a skillful manager, she might, under the right circumstances, be able to retain David while also preserving the morale of his peers. But her company's policies will stand in her way. To take the action that she believes to be in the company's best interests, she must force it awkwardly into the framework of her stack ranking system, sending unintended messages to her staff. When the rankings are leaked to the staff, or David brags to his friends about his raise, they will feel certain that they have been treated unjustly. Kate, they will assume, has either broken the rules and violated their trust, or she is a terrible judge of talent.

Incommensurability

Thus far, Kate has dealt only with engineers, but her troubles will multiply when she factors in the accountants, buyers, executive assistants, and customer service representatives. If the rewards allocable to each group will flow from the same finite pool of resources, how will she rank her top accountant against her top engineer? For the same reasons that the contributions of Ajax and Odysseus defy comparison, Kate's employees cannot be ranked along a single axis. To the extent that an employee differentiation system forces such a ranking, it necessarily undermines community.

Even in the absence of a strict differentiation regime, Kate will find it necessary to allocate rewards disparately across her various employee groups. Because she will be unable to articulate merit-based grounds for many of her decisions, she may find it difficult to obtain the buy-in of her staff. Conversely, as we will see, the sense of community among Kate's employees may be damaged to the extent that her non-merit-based decisions are perceived as evaluations of relative merit (i.e., as rewards).

Naturally, the challenges are greatest in this regard where employee groups are easily identifiable, contribute to their organizations in incommensurable ways, and are rewarded in highly disparate manners. For this reason, our last scenario must take place on a university campus:

Scenario 7: Cassandra, the president of a state university, is faced with a 15 percent budget cut due to a shortfall in tax revenue. Institutional research tells her that unhappy faculty members are more likely than unhappy staff members to leave for other institutions. Further, faculty members, who have highly specialized skills, are generally more difficult, and more expensive, to replace. Accordingly, Cassandra announces her decision to hold the salaries of the faculty constant while laying off and cutting the salaries of the staff. She is awakened the next morning by an angry mob chanting, "Less pay? No way!"

Understandably, the staff is unhappy with the news. But the reason for their unhappiness runs deeper than their pocketbooks. Cassandra's decision is unfair, it seems to them. The staff is inclined to frame the decision in terms of merit: What have we done to deserve lower pay? And what has the faculty done to deserve higher pay at our expense?

Perhaps, like Ajax, the staff members are too loyal for their own good; they have been called upon to make a sacrifice because their leader knows they will. But Cassandra's decision had nothing to do with individual employee merit. She did not intend to punish the staff or to reward the faculty, but merely to serve the best interests of the university.

Even so, the staff has good reason to be skeptical. Staff members know that they contribute to the university's mission in ways that are incommensurable with the contributions of the faculty. If their respective contributions were compared, as the staff assumes they must have been, someone will have had to make a value judgment. And which does the university value more? The solid, reliable work of the loyal and accountable staff member, or the less reliable but occasionally brilliant work of the mercurial professor?

The staff knows the answer. The functions most central to the university's mission are those performed by the faculty. Those employees directly carrying out the university's teaching and research agenda are the most likely recipients of high salaries and public recognition because their jobs are more closely aligned with the things the university was established to do. Indeed, to the extent the public university funnels resources into areas dominated by staff, taxpayers are likely to see it as waste and inefficiency. The taxpayers have a point, as the staff generally serves to support the faculty, which is on the front lines of delivering most of the services that the public wants from a university. In this sense, the staff is merely an overhead cost. Under budget pressure from taxpayers and legislators, some universities may go as far as to decide that they should spend what it takes to attract first-rate faculty, while they can get away with second-rate staff.

Businesses operate in much the same way, often reserving resources for employees working closest to profit centers and in departments central to their value propositions. This means that the back-office work of accountants, lawyers, human resources professionals, and administrative personnel tends to be viewed as secondary to the work of salesmen, engineers, and general managers. Few complex human endeavors are without this sort of hierarchy. In opera, as Flamand insists in *Capriccio*, the rule has often been "prima la musica—dopo le parole."[45] Words may precede music in time and help to inspire composers, but it is the music that draws the crowds and the composers' names that we remember.

Thus, to the faculty, the salesmen, and the composers go most of the laurels, and perhaps rightly so. But what is a corporation without its contracts and ledgers, or an opera without its libretto? We need both words and music, chorus and prima donna, to carry off an opera. We must be able to show those in support roles that we value their contributions. They must ultimately feel that justice is served, or our organizations will cease to function properly.

Leadership without Rules

The librettist knows that he loses the popularity contest with the composer not on the merits of his own work but rather on the general preference of the public for music over lyric. Many of the differences in rewards between employee groups result from the operation of the free market, and even the jilted librettist may concede that the public should allocate its resources according to its preferences.

Still, the librettist, the university staff member, and the corporate accountant cannot help feeling wronged. Justice is strained when Ajax competes with Odysseus for rewards. In these cases, it is the manager's job to keep the team together. When managers make difficult resource allocation decisions, they must be able to convince their employees that they are acting in the best interests of their organization. This, no doubt, requires some degree of trust. Employees must feel that they can rely on their managers to navigate a complex environment of many considerations and limited resources to arrive at just, if imperfect, outcomes.

Good managers understand the power of rewards to build and destroy community. Accordingly, they reward good work while also fostering an environment of respect, compassion, and moderation. They encourage competition when it is healthy and discourage it when it is not. They play up rewards where they have the power to incentivize good behavior and understate rewards where they threaten to undermine community. Good managers do not attempt to reduce management to axioms, systems, and buzzwords because they know that critical particulars would then slip between the cracks. They know that management is an art, not a science—that there is no such thing as the "one best way" for all situations.

The implementation of systems like the General Schedule and 20-70-10 betrays a fundamental lack of trust in managers. While Congress worries that managers will differentiate too much, and on the wrong bases, private companies worry that managers will not differentiate enough. In the former case, no room is left for rewards, and, in the latter case, no room is left for anything else. Forced differentiation systems may impose rigor on weak managers, requiring that they allocate resources carefully. And the General Schedule may ensure some degree of neutrality in the civil service. But, as we have seen, strict rules in both categories rob good managers of the flexibility they need to build and maintain strong teams. Justice and its utilitarian concomitants are too important, and too complex, to be left to formulas.

To do away with some of the rules, systems, and procedures is to ask more of managers—that they think independently, take responsibility for their decisions, and stand firm without policies at which to point while shrugging their shoulders. In the absence of overly restrictive rules, managers are free to act on their own insight and good judgment. To some, this is too great a burden; to others, it is an opportunity to lead. For those in the latter category, rules can be no substitute. As particularism implies, and as long experience shows, leadership can succeed where rules are bound to fail.

* * *

C. Cale McDowell is an attorney practicing in the corporate and international sections of Jackson Walker L.L.P. From 2006 to 2009, he served as Paul Woodruff's principal deputy in the School of Undergraduate Studies at the University of Texas at Austin.

Works Cited in the Afterword

Bracken, D. W., C. W. Timmreck, and A. H. Church, eds. (2000). *The Handbook of Multisource Feedback*. San Francisco: Jossey-Bass.

Butler, Samuel, trans. (1898). *The Iliad of Homer*. London: Longmans, Green, and Co.

Cardozo, Benjamin (1921). *The Nature of the Judicial Process*. New Haven, Conn.: Yale University Press.

Hughes, Daniel J., ed. (1993). *Moltke on the Art of War: Selected Writings*. New York: Presidio Press.

Kilcullen, David (2010). *Counterinsurgency*. New York: Oxford.

Levett, M. J., revised by M. Burnyeat (1990). *The Theaetetus of Plato*. Indianapolis: Hackett.

Mamet, David (2002). *Glengarry Glen Ross*. Zupnick Cinema Group. Film.

Mayo, Elton (1933). *The Human Problems of an Industrial Civilization*. New York: Macmillan.

Meineck, Peter, trans. (2000). Aristophanes. *Clouds*. Indianapolis: Hackett.

Menand, Louis (2002). *The Metaphysical Club: A Story of Ideas in America*. New York: Farrar, Straus and Giroux.

Milkovich, George T., and Alexandra K. Wigdor, eds. (1991). *Pay for Performance: Evaluating Performance Appraisal and Merit Pay*. Washington, D.C.: National Academy Press.

Petraeus, David H., and James F. Amos. (2006). *Army/Marine Corps Field Manual 3-24, Counterinsurgency*. Washington, D.C.: Government Printing Office.

Posner, Richard A. (2003). *Law, Pragmatism, and Democracy*. Cambridge, Mass.: Harvard University Press.

——— (2008). *How Judges Think*. Cambridge, Mass.: Harvard University Press.

Taylor, F. W. (1911). *The Principles of Scientific Management*. New York: Harper and Brothers.

Weber, Max (1946). *From Max Weber*. Translated by H. H. Gerth and C. Wright Mills New York: Oxford University Press.

Welch, J., with S. Welch (2005). *Winning*. New York: HarperCollins.

Notes

1. Aristophanes, *Clouds*, 222–233, as translated in Meineck (2000), pp. 18–19.
2. Levett (1990), p. 301.
3. Oliver Wendell Holmes, "Ideals and Doubts," in Holmes, *Collected Legal Papers*, pp. 303, 306 (1920 [1915]), quoted in Posner (2008).
4. Cardozo (1921), pp. 166–167, quoting from G. Lowes Dickinson, *Religion and Immortality*, p. 70.

5. Oliver Wendell Holmes to Elmer Gertz, March 1, 1899, Gertz Papers, Library of Congress; quoted in Menand (2002), p. 342.

6. *Lochner v. New York*, 198 U.S. 45, 76 (1905) (Holmes, J., dissenting).

7. See note 5, above.

8. Posner (2003), pp. 351–352.

9. Ibid.

10. Thersites is many things to many people, but he was never a model employee. In the *Iliad*, he slanders and attempts to undermine Agamemnon. Later, he appears in Goethe's *Faust* in the form of the composite character Zoilo-Thersites, declaring, "Das Tiefe hoch, das Hohe tief / Das Schiefe grad, das Grade schief / Das ganz allein macht mich gesund / So will ich's auf dem Erdenrund" (lines 5467–5470, translated in verse by A. S. Kline as follows: "When low is high, and high is low / bent is straight, and straight not so / that alone fills me with mirth / I wish it so throughout the Earth"). Shakespeare gives us perhaps the clearest view of Thersites' instinct for producing outcomes against the interests of his superiors. In *Troilus and Cressida*, Thersites tells Ajax, "I would thou didst itch from head to foot and I had the scratching of thee; I would make thee the loathsomest scab in Greece."

11. Thea von Harbou, *Metropolis* (London: Readers Library, 1927).

12. Homer, *The Iliad*, Book 4, as translated in Butler (1898), p. 59.

13. See Hughes (1993).

14. Kilcullen (2010), p. 34.

15. Petraeus and Amos (2006), sec. 1–157.

16. Taylor (1911), pp. 40, 137.

17. Ibid., p. 59.

18. Ibid.

19. Ibid., p. 42.

20. Ibid., p. 59.

21. Ibid., p. 46.

22. Ibid., p. 37.

23. Practitioners of lean manufacturing and other methodologies deriving efficiency from time and motion study will find Taylor's work somewhat familiar.

24. See Mayo (1933).

25. Weber (1946), p. 228.

26. Petraeus and Amos (2006), sec. 7–0.

27. Shari Ballard as told to George Anders, "Management Leaders Turn Attention to Followers," *Wall Street Journal*, December 24, 2007, http://online.wsj.com/article/SB119844629771347563-email.html.

28. Bharat Mediratta as told to Julie Bick, "The Google Way: Give Engineers Room," *New York Times*, October 21, 2007, http://www.nytimes.com/2007/10/21/jobs/21pre.html.

29. Ibid.

30. For general discussion of multisource feedback, see Bracken et al. (2000).

31. Plutarch, *Lives of the Noble Greeks and Romans*, Life of Pyrrhus 21:9.

32. See Kilcullen (2010), p. 57.

33. Milkovich and Wigdor (1991), p. 15.

34. See 5 *Code of Federal Regulations* §531.404.

35. Milkovich and Wigdor (1991), p. 14 (citing H. Kaufman, *The Growth of the Federal Personnel System*, p. 106 in the American Assembly, *The Federal Government Service* [New York: Columbia University Press, 1954]).

36. This was the view of Franklin Roosevelt, for example, who urged his agencies to look outside the civil service for employees who would be more responsive to his policy agenda. See Milkovich and Wigdor (1991), pp. 15, 17.

37. See *Elevating Our Federal Workforce: Chief Human Capital Officers Offer Advice to President Obama*, a report prepared by the Partnership for Public Service and Grant Thornton LLP, 2008.

38. In a recent study, a randomly selected group of employees at the University of California were informed about a website listing the salaries of all university employees. A subsequent survey revealed an asymmetric response among employees who were informed about the website, with employees whose salaries were below the median for their departments reporting lower job satisfaction and employees whose salaries were above the median reporting no higher satisfaction. Hence, the overall effect of the employees' access to salary information was lower job satisfaction. See David E. Card,

Alexandre Mas, Enrico Moretti, and Emmanuel Saez, *Inequality at Work: The Effect of Peer Salaries on Job Satisfaction* (September 2010), NBER Working Paper Series, Vol. w16396, available at SSRN, http://ssrn.com/abstract=1683166.

39. See note 37, above.
40. Welch (2005), p. 42.
41. Mamet (2002).
42. Welch (2005), p. 37.
43. "The Struggle to Measure Performance," *BusinessWeek*, January 9, 2006, http://www.businessweek.com/magazine/content/06_02/b3966060.htm.
44. Welch (2005), p. 42.
45. Richard Strauss, *Capriccio* (1942), translated by Maria Massey for the Juilliard Opera Theatre.

BIBLIOGRAPHY

*Unless indicated otherwise, all translations are my own. For Ovid, I have used
Lombardo; for Ajax I generally use Meineck.*

Angle, Stephen C. (2009). *Sagehood: The Contemporary Significance of Neo-
Confucian Philosophy.* New York: Oxford University Press.

Badaracco, Joseph L., Jr. (2002). *Leading Quietly: An Unorthodox Guide to
Doing the Right Thing.* Boston: Harvard Business School Press.

Bett, Richard (1989). "The Sophists and Relativism." *Phronesis* 34, 139–169.

Brody, Baruch (1982). "Towards a Theory of Respect for Persons." *Tulane
Studies in Philosophy* 31, 61–76.

Brown, Michael E., and Treviño, Linda K. (2006) "Ethical Leadership: A
Review and Future Directions." *Leadership Quarterly* 17, 595–616.

Burns, James MacGregor (1978). *Leadership.* New York: Harper and Row.

Chin, Annping (2007). *The Authentic Confucius: A Life of Thought and Politics.*
New York: Scribner.

Cawthorn, Drew (2002). *Philosophical Foundations of Leadership.* New
Brunswick, N.J.: Transaction Publishers.

Ciulla, Joanne, Terry L. Price, and Susan E. Murphy, eds. (2005). *The Quest for
Moral Leaders: Essays on Leadership Ethics.* Cheltenham: Edward Elgar.

Ciulla, Joanne B. (2003). *The Ethics of Leadership.* Belmont, Calif.: Wadsworth/
Thomson.

Cohen, G. A. (1997). "Where the Action Is: On the Site of Distributive Justice."
Philosophy and Public Affairs 26, 3–30.

——— (2008). *Rescuing Justice and Equality.* Cambridge, Mass.: Harvard
University Press.

Crisp, Roger (2007). "Ethics without Reasons?" *Journal of Moral Philosophy* 4,
40–49.

Dancy, Jonathan (2004). *Ethics without Principles.* Oxford: Clarendon Press.

Darwall, Stephen (1977). "Two Kinds of Respect." *Ethics* 88, 36–49.

Folger, Robert, and Russell Cropanzano (1998). *Organizational Justice and Human Resource Management*. Thousand Oaks, Calif.: Sage.

Frankfurt, Harry (1999). "Equality and Respect," in his *Necessity, Volition, and Love*. Cambridge: Cambridge University Press, 146–54.

Gagarin, Michael, and Paul Woodruff, eds. (1995). *Early Greek Political Thought from Homer to the Sophists*. Cambridge: Cambridge University Press.

Gert, Bernard (2005). "Moral Arrogance and Moral Theories." *Nous, Philosophical Issues* 15: *Normativity*, 368–385.

Greenberg, Jerald (2002). *Managing Behavior in Organizations*. Upper Saddle River, N.J.: Prentice Hall.

Griswold, Charles (2007). *Forgiveness: A Philosophical Exploration*. Cambridge: Cambridge University Press.

Hamburger, Philip (1946). "The Great Judge." Life Magazine, November 4, 1946, 122 and 125. http://books.google.com/books?id=tUwEAAAAMB AJ&pg=PA116&source=gbs_toc_r&cad=2#v=onepage&q&f=false.

Hayford, Harrison, and Merton Sealts, eds. (1962). *Billy Budd, Sailor (An Inside Narrative) by Herman Melville*. Chicago: University of Chicago Press.

Herring, George C. (1979). *America's Longest War: The United States and Vietnam 1950–1975*. New York: John Wiley and Sons.

Hill, Thomas E. Jr. (2000). *Respect, Pluralism, and Justice*. Oxford: Oxford University Press.

Hovland, Michele (2010). "Reintegration of National Guard Soldiers with Post-traumatic Stress Disorder." Student research paper for the U.S. Army War College, Carlisle Barracks. http://handle.dtic.mil/100.2/ADA521761.

Hursthouse, Rosalind (1990). "After Hume's Justice." *Proceedings of the Aristotelian Society* 91, 229–245.

Johnson, Craig E. (2011). *Meeting the Ethical Challenges of Leadership: Casting Light or Shadow*. Fourth Edition. Thousand Oaks, Calif.: Sage.

Keegan, John (1987). *The Mask of Command*. Harmondsworth: Penguin Books.

Knox, Bernard (1979). "The *Ajax* of Sophocles." In his *Word and Action: Essays on the Ancient Theater*, pp. 125–160. Baltimore: Johns Hopkins University Press.

Konstan, David (2001). *Pity Transformed*. London: Duckworth.

Kraut, Richard (2007). *What Is Good and Why: The Ethics of Well-Being*. Cambridge, Mass.: Harvard University Press.

Lawrence, Mark A. (2008). *The Vietnam War: A Concise International History*. New York: Oxford University Press.

Lombardo, Stanley (2010). *Ovid: Metamorphoses*. Indianapolis: Hackett.

Lucas, John (1966). *The Principles of Politics*. Oxford: Clarendon Press.

—— (1980). *Justice*. Oxford: Oxford University Press.

MacIntyre, Alasdair (1988). *Whose Justice? Which Rationality?* London: Duckworth.

Margalit, Avishai (1996). *The Decent Society*. Translated by Naomi Goldblum. Cambridge, Massachusetts: Harvard University Press.

Meineck, Peter, and Paul Woodruff (2007). *Sophocles: Four Tragedies, Ajax Women of Trachis, Electra, Philoctetes*. Indianapolis: Hackett.

Nussbaum, Martha (2006). *Frontiers of Justice: Disability, Nationality, Species Membership*. Cambridge, Mass.: Belknap Press of Harvard University Press.

Pogge, Thomas (2007). *John Rawls: His Life and Theory of Justice*. Translated from the German edition of 1994 by Michelle Kosch. New York: Oxford University Press.

Rath, Tom, and Barry Conchie (2008). *Strengths Based Leadership: Great Leaders, Teams, and Why People Follow*. New York: Gallup Press.

Rawls, John (1971). *A Theory of Justice*. Cambridge, Mass.: Harvard University Press.

—— (2001). *Justice as Fairness: A Restatement*. Edited by Erin Kelly. Cambridge, Mass.: Belknap Press of Harvard University Press.

—— (2005). *Political Liberalism*. Expanded edition. New York: Columbia University Press.

Raz, Joseph (1990). "Facing Diversity: The Case for Epistemic Abstinence." *Philosophy and Public Affairs* 19, 3–46.

Rousseau, Denise M. (1995). *Psychological Contracts in Organizations: Understanding Written and Unwritten Agreements*. Thousand Oaks, Calif.: Sage.

Sandel, Michael J. (2009). *Justice: What's the Right Thing to Do?* New York: Farrar, Straus and Giroux.

Sen, Amartya (2009). *The Idea of Justice*. Cambridge, Mass.: Belknap Press of Harvard University Press.

Shay, Jonathan (1994). *Achilles in Vietnam: Combat Trauma and the Undoing of Character*. New York: Simon and Schuster.

Sheppard, Blair H., Roy J. Lewicki, and John W. Minton (1992). *Organizational Justice: The Search for Fairness in the Workplace*. New York: Lexington Books.

Singer, M. (1997). *Ethics and Justice in Organizations: A Normative-Empirical Dialogue*. Aldershot: Avebury.

Slingerland, Edward (2003). *Confucius: Analects; With Selections from Traditional Commentaries*. Indianapolis: Hackett.

Stafford, William (2003). *Every War Has Two Losers*. Minneapolis, Minn.: Milkweed Editions.

Temkin, Larry (1993). *Inequality*. New York: Oxford University Press.

Väyrynen, Pekka (2006). "Moral Generalism: Enjoy in Moderation." *Ethics* 116, 707–741.

Vasiliou, Iakovos (2008). *Aiming at Virtue in Plato*. Cambridge: Cambridge University Press.

Walumbwa, Fred O., Bruce J. Avolio, William L. Gardner, Tara S. Wernsing, and Suzanne J. Peterson (2008). "Authentic Leadership: Development and Validation of a Theory-Based Measure." *Journal of Management* 34, 89.

Wiggins, David (2006). "Neo-Aristotelian Reflections on Justice." In his *Ethics: Twelve Lectures on the Philosophy of Morality*, pp. 269–324. Cambridge, Mass.: Harvard University Press.

Williams, Bernard (1980). "Justice as a Virtue." In Amelie Rorty, ed., *Essays on Aristotle's Ethics,* pp. 189–199. Berkeley: University of California Press.

——— (1993). *Shame and Necessity*. Berkeley: University of California Press.

Woodruff, Paul (2001). *Reverence: Renewing a Forgotten Virtue*. New York: Oxford University Press.

——— (2005). *First Democracy: The Challenge of an Ancient Idea*. New York: Oxford University Press.

—— (2008). *The Necessity of Theater: The Art of Watching and Being Watched.* New York: Oxford University Press.

—— (Forthcoming). "Justice as a Virtue of the Soul." To be inclided in a festschrift for Julia Annas.

Wren, Thomas J., Ronald E. Riggio, and Michael A. Genovese, eds. (2009). *Leadership and the Liberal Arts: Achieving the Promise of a Liberal Education.* New York: Palgrave Macmillan.

Yingling, Paul (2007). "A Failure of Generalship." *Armed Forces Journal*, May 2007. http://www.armedforcesjournal.com/2007/05/2635198/.

INDEX